DREAMING WITH
POLAR BEARS

"In this remarkable book, Dawn Brunke reminds us that we exist within an interconnected oneness of depth, beauty, and awareness—if only we wake up, look around, and listen. Lucid dreaming helps us experience deeper connections in a life-altering way and recognize the living awareness of other species, our shared planet, and the vast universe. *Dreaming with Polar Bears* encourages us all to wake up, remember, and understand this ancient knowledge."

ROBERT WAGGONER, AUTHOR OF *LUCID DREAMING:
GATEWAY TO THE INNER SELF*

"Right from the introduction you will be drawn in, fascinated by Dawn Brunke's exploration of conscious dreaming and her ability to deeply communicate with animals. Her enthralling exploration will explode your awareness into new possibilities. Read and dream on."

PENELOPE SMITH, ANIMAL COMMUNICATION SPECIALIST
AND AUTHOR OF *ANIMAL TALK*, *WHEN ANIMALS SPEAK*,
AND *ANIMALS IN SPIRIT*

"More than once I've fallen into the arms of Dawn Brunke's books with joyful delight, and *Dreaming with Polar Bears* has had me falling all over again. The author is a wise guide of oft-hidden transhistorical traditions. She gives us all a much needed reminder of how to restore our connections to the vital realities of the dreaming world and the world of dreaming."

SIMON BUXTON, AUTHOR OF *THE SHAMANIC WAY OF THE BEE*

"Dawn Brunke's extraordinary gift of openness to the ancient ways of communication with the animal world opens new horizons to explore the interconnectedness of all life. Her polar bear dreams invite us to stop: to open our eyes, feel, listen, and remember; to allow ourselves to be vulnerable and open our hearts to share with all that is. May this book remind us that we are part of nature and how living that reality can bring a meaningful and balanced life."

HRH PRINCESS IRENE OF THE NETHERLANDS,
AUTHOR OF *SCIENCE, SOUL, AND THE SPIRIT OF NATURE* AND
DIALOGUE WITH NATURE

"This book is a must for anyone interested in lucid dreaming and developing relationships with teachers in the spirit world through dreams. It asks deep questions and offers unique answers gleaned from a lifetime of dream experiences."

NICKI SCULLY, AUTHOR OF *POWER ANIMAL MEDITATIONS* AND
PLANETARY HEALING: SPIRIT MEDICINE
FOR GLOBAL TRANSFORMATION

"Dawn Brunke has taken time to listen deeply to what has called her. She helps us to awaken, to open our being, to recover the sacred covenant of our vocation as custodians of the planet to become co-creators and co-dreamers with the many beings on, below, and above our Earth of a new dream sourced from the heart. I cannot think of a more important message for our time."

VERONICA GOODCHILD, PH.D., FACULTY AT
PACIFICA GRADUATE INSTITUTE AND AUTHOR OF
EROS AND CHAOS AND *SONGLINES OF THE SOUL*

DREAMING WITH
POLAR BEARS

Spirit Journeys with Animal Guides

DAWN BAUMANN BRUNKE

Bear & Company
Rochester, Vermont • Toronto, Canada

Bear & Company
One Park Street
Rochester, Vermont 05767
www.BearandCompanyBooks.com

Text stock is SFI certified

Bear & Company is a division of Inner Traditions International

Library of Congress Cataloging-in-Publication Data
Brunke, Dawn Baumann.
  Dreaming with polar bears : spirit journeys with animal guides / Dawn Baumann
Brunke.
      pages cm
  Includes bibliographical references.
  Summary: "A guide to co-dreaming with animals for personal and planetary
evolution"— Provided by publisher.
  ISBN 978-1-59143-183-1 (pbk.) — ISBN 978-1-59143-763-5 (e-book)
  1. Animals—Miscellanea. 2. Dreams. 3. Polar bear—Miscellanea. I. Title.
  BF1623.A55B78 2014
  133.8'9—dc23
                                                        2014009992

Printed and bound in the United States by Lake Book Manufacturing, Inc.
The text stock is SFI certified. The Sustainable Forestry Initiative® program
promotes sustainable forest management.

10   9   8   7   6   5   4   3   2   1

Text design by Debbie Glogover and layout by Virginia Scott Bowman
This book was typeset in Garamond Premier Pro with Graphite and Gill Sans
used as display typefaces

Excerpt from "The Return Journey" by Robert Moss from *Dreamways of the
Iroquois* used by permission of Inner Traditions • Bear & Company, www
.InnerTraditions.com.

To send correspondence to the author of this book, mail a first-class letter to the
author c/o Inner Traditions • Bear & Company, One Park Street, Rochester, VT
05767, and we will forward the communication, or contact the author directly at
www.animalvoices.net.

Contents

PART 3

Coming Home

�422ᴉ

Acknowledgments

Thank you Phil Kotofskie for all your helpful comments over the years and, once again, with this book. Thanks Patricia Wade and Carol Baumann for reading the first draft. Thank you Tayria Ward for generously sharing insights and contacts and Betsy Robinson for listening and laughing.

Thanks to my publisher, Inner Traditions; you make the process easy! Thanks to intuitive gatekeeper Jon Graham as well as Jeanie Levitan and Cynthia More. Thanks Kelly Bowen, Jessie Wimett, Manzanita Carpenter, Blythe Bates, and the ever helpful John Hays. Thanks to text designers Debbie Glogover and Virginia Scott Bowman. Thank you Erica Robinson for all your persistence and help and Peri Ann Swan for a perfect cover. And big thanks to my editor, Jamaica Burns Griffin, and copyeditor Elizabeth Wilson for clarity, consistency, and grammatical precision.

Thanks to those who spent time reading my manuscript and offering kind words of support: Robert Waggoner, Robert Moss, Irene van Lippe, Penelope Smith, Veronica Goodchild, Simon Buxton, and Nicki Scully.

Thank you Bob and Alyeska for all the love and laughter and dog pals Barney, Zak, Max, and Riza for inspiring us to live life with an open heart.

Thanks to dreamworld friends, guides, and guardians who continue to offer insights, challenges, and encouragement.

Lastly, grateful thanks to all the Polar Bear people, those in physical bodies and those in spirit, and especially Bering Strait—wise polar bear, witty friend, and co-dreamer extraordinaire. Thank you for this most amazing adventure, for trusting me to share our story, and for helping my words "sing with the song of Polar Bear."

The Invitation

One night many years ago, while sleeping on a ship, I became lucid within a dream. The usual tingly rush of excitement—*I am awake, inside my dream!*—flooded through me. But to stay anchored in the lucid state, I knew I must calm myself and observe.

My consciousness is divided into two screens of awareness. On one side is my sleeping body, tucked in a bed on a ship. On the other side is a small, lively dog called Little High Top. I find I can slip my attention directly into his mind. Inside his thoughts, I know all about him. I live with a family: a mother, a father, an older boy, and a young girl. I am happy and peppy and love to play. I am called Little High Top because I am only as big as a high-top sneaker. This is a joke in my family. When I first came to live with them, they sat me inside the boy's red high-top sneaker and took my photo, and that is how I got my name.

As the dreamer, I'm fascinated by this dual awareness and how I can shift so easily between the two worlds. I know I am Dawn, on the ship, dreaming this dream, but so also can I become Little High Top by sharing his consciousness. Even more fascinating is that I understand he is aware of me—he knows I am a dreaming human watching the events of his life from within his body. He seems welcoming of this connection, excited even, to share in this way.

Urging myself to remember every detail of the dream, I cough. In the same instant, Little High Top barks. It seems deliberate in a humorous way, and I feel compelled to try again and again. Whenever I cough as Dawn, Little High Top barks. (Or as I shall later consider, whenever Little High Top barks, Dawn coughs.) Is this synchronicity of sound some type of dream technique? But to what end? What does it do? My thoughts race, enthused with the many possibilities.

Time speeds up, and I watch Little High Top's life passing by. He is older now, his girl has left for college, and he is taken to an old uncle's house to live. The uncle is an artist whose small house sits on the side of a mountain cliff overlooking a rocky ocean bay. Perhaps the house is in Italy or Greece. The uncle paints and draws at a wood table beside a large picture window. Little High Top sits on the table across from him. Together they look out over dark blue water as the old man creates his art. I watch Little High Top's life pass as the old uncle dies, followed shortly by Little High Top. It was a good life filled with play and happiness and service. It was a life well lived.

I wrote the dream in my journal and recounted it to several people who shared my enthusiasm for the creative wonders of dreams. At the time, I was writing a book about shapeshifting with animals, focusing on what it is like to experience the world through an animal's perspective. The dream symology of two screens of awareness, along with the dreamer's ability to shift between them, accurately portrayed my experience of shapeshifting, or as I often thought about it, the ability to shift the shape of one's consciousness and thus perceive in a different way.

I found it remarkable that Little High Top knew I was a dreaming human watching his life events from within his awareness. In this sense, he seemed very much his own dog—not just a representation of some part of me but rather a sentient being visiting my dreamworld. The cough-bark connection was also intriguing. The sound came from our throats, possibly indicating the importance of creative expression and voicing oneself to the world. That we coughed and barked simultaneously represented a deeper link between us, perhaps a joining of expressive abilities. I loved the dream; it held a playful, perplexing quality that spoke to me.

Time passed, however, and other dreams were dreamed. Thus Little High Top might have simply remained an interesting journal entry, an unusual lucid experience sometimes recalled on special occasions—if it wasn't for a second dream that occurred about a year later.

I am in a small airplane flying from Juneau to Anchorage. I am sitting in the window seat, the middle seat is empty, and an older, distinguished-looking gentleman is in the aisle seat. He tells me he is a visiting professor of dreamology and that he has come to Alaska to teach a special type of dreaming. There is something old-world and charming about the man. He exudes a humble, unassuming presence, yet I sense he knows secrets.

During a lull in our conversation, I lean my forehead against the window and look outside. When we left Juneau it was dark, but now we are flying above billowy white clouds tinged early-morning gold and pink. The effect is magical and my thoughts start to drift. I imagine what it would be like to float among the clouds or even to become a cloud. It strikes me how easily my consciousness can travel to the world outside the plane. And how such a different world—one of subdued lighting and sleepy travelers and my physical body—remains inside the plane. Isn't it odd that two very different worlds can coexist so close together, separated only by a pane of glass? Isn't it peculiar how easy it is to move between them, and yet most of the time we don't acknowledge this or even believe it possible?

Suddenly, I remember the dream of Little High Top. I feel the same sensation of dual screens of awareness—which now causes me to realize that I am awake! Within my dream!

The familiar rush of excitement courses through me. Here I am, dreaming that I am sitting in an airplane—next to a professor of dreamology!—observing the way we separate different worlds of awareness, as well as remembering a dream in which I moved between two such worlds. The moment is filled with heightened possibilities. But it is fragile, too, and I know I must not lose myself in my own excitement. Still, I can't help blurting out to the professor, "I just remembered my dream!"

He turns to me with a smile and nods. Settling into his seat, he closes his eyes as I recount the dream of Little High Top. I explain how I awoke within that dream to dual awareness and how I ventured into the dog's consciousness to learn of his life, reliving key events with him as he grew older, leaving one home for another, until both he and the old uncle died.

When I tell the professor that's it, the end of the dream, he opens his eyes and looks into mine. "Is Little High Top real?"

"It was a dream," I say. (Alas, I am no longer lucid. At some point in relating the dream to the professor the edge of lucid awareness dissolved.) But he continues to question me in a good-natured way, encouraging me to consider the reality of a dog called Little High Top who lived such a life.

I begin to feel nervous. On the one hand it was just a dream, but I feel a growing sense of unease. Because a professor of dreamology persists in asking me if a dream dog is real, I am nudged into feeling something more must be involved. Suddenly he coughs and, quite involuntarily, I laugh. The actions trigger my memory of the cough-bark connection within the other dream. And I almost remember something very important. The professor leans forward and digs out a battered, dark brown leather case from under the seat in front of him. From the case, he pulls a packet of photos held together by a red rubber band. Riffling through them, he hands me one. It's a picture of a small dog—perhaps a terrier—who looks very much like Little High Top. I nod yes, this is the same type of dog, and he indicates I should turn over the photo. On the back, in a loopy handwritten script, are the words Little High Top.

Is this a trick? My heart pounds faster; my thoughts race. How could this man—is he really a professor? of dreamology?—who just happened to be sitting next to me know I would even remember this dream or recount it to him? He shows me other photos: the family, the high-top sneaker, the uncle, the table, and the window that overlooks the sea. He taps the images repeatedly with his forefinger, as if to say, See? This is real! He tells me he is returning from his brother's funeral—that his brother was the old uncle in my dream, his niece the mother in Little High Top's family.

The professor then tells me I did well in recalling the details of the dream, except the uncle did not live in Europe but in Juneau. Did I not remember the spectacular mountaintop view of the bay?

For the second time in this dream, I realize I am dreaming. I tell myself that I am in a dream and, within this world, all the professor is telling me is true. Still, there is part of me that wants to question, how is this possible? Is my dream really real? Am I connected to this dog? What does this mean? As if reading my thoughts, the professor holds up his hand and stops me with a look.

Just then—in that fast-forward way of dreams—we have landed. Everyone is bustling about, reaching into the overhead bins, gathering belongings. I stand beside the professor, who reaches into his pocket and hands me an ivory-colored card.

The paper is thick and elegant, folded crisply at the top—an invitation. I understand it is my recollection of Little High Top that allows the professor to present me this card. I understand it is a special invitation, one that involves a challenge that I am free to accept or not. As I open the card and begin to read, the professor moves closer.

"Dreaming with polar bears," he whispers in my ear.

There are dreams, and then there are *dreams*. As I scrambled to record the details of this dream in my journal, I marveled over its intricacies: the engaging story line, the humor (a professor of dreamology?), the recurrence of the dual screen of awareness, the lucid memory of a dream within a dream, and the invitation—the challenge—to dream another kind of dream. I was amazed how one dream could so cleverly build upon another, making use of dream symbology that was over a year old.

The professor's persistent attempt to prove the reality of a dog called Little High Top was also impressive. I remembered that dream and how, from the dog's perspective, I sensed he was aware of me as a dreaming human. But did this mean the dog was real in the same way

I am real? Was he asleep somewhere in our world, dreaming about a human sharing his awareness? If the other dreamer was a person I knew, I could call her up and ask, did you dream this dream too? And we could laugh, or marvel, at the chances of this shared dream ability. But how would I ever find this dog—and did the dog actually have a waking world outside the dream? Was he dreaming me? How could I know? Where does one reality end and another begin?

Such questions are not new. More than two thousand years ago the Taoist philosopher Chuang Tzu dreamed he was a butterfly, flitting and fluttering, happy to do as he pleased. Then he awoke and there he was, a man called Chuang Tzu. But which experience was real? And how could he know? The mystery of consciousness he posed is this: Am I Chuang Tzu who dreamed I was a butterfly, or am I butterfly dreaming I am Chuang Tzu?

I have always been interested in such questions. Peering through my dreams—especially lucid dreams—lurks a dreamer filled with both wonder and incredulity. Sometimes I think my dreams deliberately play with my consciousness, poking fun at my skepticism and self-doubt, urging me to consider other possibilities, to try on new ways of being.

As with most anything in life, the more attention we focus on our dreams—remembering them in the morning, recording them, telling them to others, sketching or painting them, acting in some way upon the wisdom or messages received—the more our dreams respond. We establish a dialogue between our waking and dreaming worlds, a dialogue rich in images, intelligent in symbology, helpful in insight, encouragement, or healing, and uniquely suited to our particular needs. A gateway opens.

For me, that gateway opened as I was handed the invitation. Dreaming with polar bears—even the phrasing seemed an entryway, a mysterious, poetic portal. For while it is one thing to dream about polar bears or dogs or dolphins, to dream *with* another species conveys something quite different indeed. How does one dream with polar bears? And why polar bears? Why not continue the canine connection already established within the dream? Although I live in Alaska and certainly admire the great white bears of the Far North, I had never seen a polar bear in the wild. Why not ravens or moose? Why not Chuang Tzu's butterfly?

In my imagination, it is at this point the dream professor once again holds up his hand and stops me with a look. Such questions will not take us far. To interpret, analyze, or question a dream can seem helpful at times, yet we remain strangers to the dream. To know a dream, something more is required of us. All that a dream offers in the way of ingenious hints, puzzles, visions, challenges, messages, secrets—all manner of invitation—pales next to the question, *Do you accept?*

I did. And I began to dream of polar bears. The dreams consisted of one simple, repeated scene: I am in the high Arctic, walking beside a polar bear. Although the land, sky, and seascape changed from dream to dream, the core event remained the same.

The dreams continued for almost a year, though sporadic—from two or three times a week to once every three or four weeks. Unlike my other dreams that sprawled with action and events and colorful characters, the polar bear dreams felt like hard little seeds. They held a unique quality, though what this quality was I could not exactly say. I was not lucid inside the dreams, but I sensed a growing awareness within.

In waking life, I worked with the dreams. I wrote them down; I drew sketches; I retold the dream as if I were the bear, the landscape, a disinterested observer. I tried to reenter the dream in meditation, to question the dream bear, to engage the help of a dream guide, or to find some symbolic clue or pattern as to why this particular dream was recurring. But it was as if the dreams were encased by a protective coating, a barrier not easily yielding to any of my preferred dream techniques, nor any I found in books.

Clearly, there are times to persist and times to yield. I felt it best to leave the dreams be, to simply experience them, allowing them to unfold naturally. What else could be done? Then, soon after I let go, something happened inside the dream that changed everything.

As usual, I walk beside the polar bear. It is night and we are traveling across a wide, flat, silvery expanse of snow. The air is crystalline, sharp and clear. I notice a rhythm in our walk, something distinct and familiar. Slowly, realizations come to me, one by one: I have been here before. This is a dream. I have dreamed this dream before. I am dreaming now. The recognition is both obvious and amusing. With a laugh, I reach out to touch the bear's shoulder and he turns his great white head to me. I realize I am quite calm, not overly excited as I usually am in lucid dreams. For a moment I want to question the bear—Why are we here? What are we doing?—but my awareness is now also within the bear. He is looking at me, into me, and I see myself through his eyes. He remembers me; he has seen me before, in his dreams. Then I realize not only am I dreaming, he is dreaming, too. We are both awake—lucid and aware—within each other's dream.

This is a book about dreaming with polar bears. It is about the many ways dreams speak to us at deep levels, urging us to awaken. It is about meeting polar bears in a different way, sharing a different reality beneath appearances. It is about how our impressions and assumptions about polar bears (or any animal) can teach us about ourselves, and how the presence of polar bears in our world speaks to something larger still. Finally, this is a book about relationship. It is about a meeting place between realities, an exploration of the dreamworld both created and discovered when two dreamers meet.

I continued to dream walk beside the polar bear. But things were different now. I was usually awake within the dreams and so, said the bear, was he. Our shared thoughts flowed through the dreams, night to night, in seamless conversation. The polar bear claimed he was a specialized dreamer, a real bear living in the Arctic who had the ability to share dreams with other dreamers. I claimed to be a real human living in Alaska who was relatively new to this way of dream connecting.

Dreaming the dreams was like living inside a fantastic novel. The bear told me what it was like to live as a polar bear, describing his den, his mother, his life as a cub. He showed me how he learned to hunt, how to smell the snow and wind to know where seals were sleeping or when storms were coming. I met the Polar Bear Council, a group of spirit bears who served as guides, facilitating shared dreaming as part of planetary evolution. They spoke of special teachings that polar bears hold for the Earth, what Native peoples call Polar Bear Medicine: the ability to consciously dream.

In order to understand polar bears, the bear said to me, *you need to become a polar bear person.* He encouraged me to visit other bears by sharing their awareness, to see and feel their life experiences as I had with the dog called Little High Top. And so I traveled in dreams and visions, shifting the shape of my consciousness from human to bear and back again.

I experienced many dreams of shared awareness, often with lucidity, and became more adept at connecting with the polar bear while both asleep and awake, for dreams can occur anytime. Sometimes, while riding in a car, walking, or simply gazing through a window, I would slip into the shared dreamscape, viewing the vast frozen Arctic landscape shimmering like a translucent curtain over the Alaskan mountains and terrain of my home.

As time went on, my relationship with the dream bear deepened and the nagging question, *Is this real?* stopped yapping through my head. My questions were larger now, as was my way of seeing the world.

I began to consider, what if the reason for the dream is not mine, but the bear's? Perhaps the bear has reasons to dream about me, to share his thoughts and life experiences with a human. Such thoughts take us outside our conventional framework of reality. To create a bridge that joins humans and polar bears in meaningful relationship is like trying to bring the full reality of a dream into waking consciousness—or the fullness of waking consciousness into a dream.

To know polar bears, we must first move beyond our idea of polar bears. Beyond the collective human concepts about polar bears— ferocious man-eater, cuddly image for children, the worried face of global warming and extinction—is the bear itself, with its life, thoughts, and dreams. To move beyond our idea of polar bears, we must be willing to move beyond our limited ideas about ourselves and our connection with others. We must be willing to allow a larger understanding of the world, a larger presence of who we are.

To truly know a dream we must feel it, breathe it, and, ultimately, allow it to live through us. When a dream calls to us, we begin with who we are. The dream speaks to us in a manner uniquely ours, whispering reminders, stirring awareness, nudging us, *Wake up, Wake up!*

This is a book about what happens when we accept an invitation from our dreams. This is a book about dreaming with polar bears.

PART I

A Personal History of Dreaming Bears

Why do they come to us, the animals?
What do they want, inhabiting our dreams?

JAMES HILLMAN, *DREAM ANIMALS*

1

The Dog in the Basement

In the beginning, before the bear, is the big white dog. She waits upon a pillow bed in the basement of my being—welcomer, protector, teacher, friend. She is the first clue, the key image, the guardian at the entrance to my personal history of dreaming.

Perhaps you are wondering why a person dreams with polar bears or writes a book about it. Was she called? Was it Polar Bear who sent the invitation to dream? Were there clues in the dreamer's life along the way? How did it begin?

When we begin to engage our dreams in meaningful ways, we soon find ourselves traveling through a multiplicity of worlds. It can be challenging to translate experiences from one world to another, to convey subtleties of contextual meaning across different arenas, through different modes of interpreting reality. As we trudge along, we find ourselves wearing different hats: scientist and artist, detective and intuitive, observer and participant. We need patience and persistence—perceptiveness, too. The journey may captivate, and soon we're frequent fliers along the cross-cultural continuum of deeper knowing. We become adventurers, exploring the psyche, mapping secret passageways, charting unknown bridges and wormholes within the multiverse.

To begin, however, a foundation is helpful. While this is not a book about cataloging or analyzing dreams, it is based on the idea that some familiarity with how we relate to our dreams is both valuable and necessary. How do we translate the unique symbols and images that appear in our inner theater? How do we find deeper meaning in what initially seems to be just a dream? How does each dream fit within the history of our dreaming lives? How may we recall and retain these stories in waking consciousness so that they speak to us—and so that we, in response, may speak to them? Indeed, as when visiting any foreign country, it's useful to learn the language and customs.

What follows in part 1 are the significant dreams I've had about bears. I share these for two reasons. First and most obvious, they answer how my polar bear dreaming began. It has been fascinating for me to gather and reclaim the dreams that appear to signify an ongoing connection with polar bears; though, this was not apparent for much of my life.

Second, the dreams serve as examples through which we can try different dream decoding techniques. It's wise to be versatile. It's smart to have a large box of dream tools, for each dream is unique. An approach that helps us one time may not be appropriate another. No one way is advocated here, no four secret steps to success. Rather, we'll try on different styles to discover what works best for each dream and consider varied ways to make meaningful connections. The following dreams are held, turned over and inside out, pondered, examined, and questioned in this spirit of playful exploration. Some views offer basic observations; others are more arcane. Some may speak to you, others not. Perhaps certain seeds will remain dormant within you for a time until their magic is needed to help you in your dreams.

In the end, when I finally met the polar bear heart to heart, mind to mind, none of this mattered. We entered a dream relationship in a completely different way. However, I don't know if this would have happened without giving a lot of attention to my dreams—recording them, sharing them, puzzling and playing and wondering about them. The incubation period was necessary. Part 2 of this book takes us into a very different world. Before we venture there, however, let us get to know the dreamworld territory. It's good to be prepared. Let us begin.

THE FIRST DREAM

The first dream I can remember occurred when I was two years old. Most likely the distinction between dreaming and waking hadn't yet lodged in place, and that's why it didn't seem like a dream at all, but a perfectly real event.

> *My parents and I go to visit some neighbors, a man and a woman. They don't have children, but the woman tells me that I can go play with the dogs in the basement. As the grown-ups walk into the living room, I climb down the basement stairs, step-by-step, alone.*
>
> *At the bottom of the stairs is an open room, and in the middle of the room is a big, white dog lying on a pillow bed. She smiles, welcoming me, and I go to lie beside her, my head near her belly. I close my eyes. When I open them, there are two more white dogs, one on either side of me. They are smaller than the first dog, but a bit bigger than me. I snuggle between the three dogs, feeling their soft fur, smelling their warm, doggy skin, and I am very happy.*
>
> *My parents call to me from halfway down the basement stairs. They tell me it is time to go home. "Or would you rather stay with the dogs?" they ask. I consider this and tell them I will stay, that I would like to live with the dogs in the basement. They laugh, as do the neighbors. Then my mother comes down the stairs, takes my hand, and leads me home.*

Several times after this event, I asked my parents if I could visit the big white dogs. I wanted to see them again, to lay with them on the pillow bed. But my parents shook their heads. They did not understand my question. Eventually I stopped asking and the incident was forgotten. Many years later, as a teenager, I remembered the dogs. Curious about this small mystery from my past, I asked my mother about the memory. She could not recall any childless neighbors with big white dogs. Even if there had been, she added, did I really think she would have allowed a two-year-old to go alone into a basement full of dogs? "It must have been a dream."

WHAT DOES IT MEAN?

When I review the history of my dream life, it is the big white dog in the basement that seems the start of everything. She is a forerunner. Since that first dream, she has appeared in different ways, in other situations. Sometimes she wears other furry disguises: a white coyote, a white fox, a white horse, a big white bear. She has also shown up in my waking life, most often assuming the form of a white dog.

Although this dream may not be my first dream, it is my first remembered dream. I have recalled it again and again over the years. In this way, it has become a personal myth—a dream of a dream. It glows softly with a warm patina, a cherished memory from my childhood. And this, too, has become part of the dream.

When I now look at this dream in a symbolic way, I first notice its structure. The child is separated from her parents, sent underground where she interacts with big white animals, and later retrieved by her human family and returned to the world aboveground. The progression of the dream brings to mind the three stages of a rite of passage: separation (a moving away from the world we know), transition or liminality (an adventure in the in-between often marked by ambiguous categories and unusual experiences), and reincorporation (a return to the world, marked by change). This dream holds all three elements.

Leaving home with her parents, the dreamer is separated from them, sent away to a room beneath the surface. She leaves what is known (her home, her parents) for the unknown (the neighbor's home, their basement). Although the idea of playing with dogs is enticing, the dreamer must venture away from her family to reach the underground room, alone.

The descent into the basement marks the beginning of transition. It's classic; down, down the dreamer goes. At the bottom, she meets a big white dog, a welcoming representative of the animal world. Basic distinctions are apparent here: the human family is above, in the "living" room; the dreamer is underground, where the animals dwell. Transitional phases are often marked by ambiguity and the merging of categories. The dog smiles at the child as a human might do; the child lies with the dogs in a heap, cuddling as a pup might do. The blending of boundaries between human and animal communing on the pillow bed seems natural here—so natural that the dreamer wants to stay, to live with the family of dogs.

In the third phase, reincorporation, the dreamer is called to return to her human family. But she is also offered a choice, to stay with the dogs in the basement. When the dreamer chooses to stay, there is laughter. This is telling. There is often something that happens in the liminal phase—a wounding, a mark, a symbolic gesture—that separates before from after. Perhaps the laughter causes the child to feel humiliation; she is laughed at for choosing what cannot be in the "real" world. Perhaps the adults laugh because they are uncomfortable with the child's choice to live with animals rather than humans, something conventional reality will not allow. No matter why, the choice and the laughter signal a change. The dreamer has declared her preference and returns to her parents not the same child who went down the basement stairs. She now carries a secret, a mystery that has yet to unfold. She has seen something—*felt* something—with the dogs that the grown-ups have not, and has been changed in the process.

The dream guides the dreamer from what is known (family, humans, neighbors) to what is unknown (basement, dogs), and back again. Through the process, the dreamer is transformed. She has been offered a gift that the aboveground people do not understand (or remember).

In some ways, every dream is a potential rite of passage. We move from the world we know while waking to an inner theater of potentiality. Sleep is our transition, our movement into the basement of our being. We even think of it as going down, as in the phrase *falling asleep*. There, in the inner world, we engage the liminal zone—a place neither here nor there. Not unconsciously asleep, yet not consciously awake, we enter a world of unlimited creation where all things are possible, subject only to the creative rules of the dream. In this sense, dreaming is a liminal state. On waking, we return to where we started: consciously present in our physical body, in a world governed by gravity and other consensual laws, to our unique set of personal circumstances. Whether we allow ourselves to carry the gift (the secret message or meaning) from the dream and open to change is our choice.

Of course, there are many ways to explore a dream, many avenues that offer different windows through which we can appreciate detailed aspects of the dream. For example, we might look at each element within a dream, decoding its symbols and the way it represents something about the dreamer.

When considering the basement, we might begin with the idea that it represents a foundation, the base from which we build the house of our personality or conscious self. The contents of the basement may thus represent our subconscious or unconscious elements, the inner or underworld of the psyche. Everyone's basement is different, and its appearance may change through time. If we dream of a basement that is shadowy or dirty, it tells us one thing. If it's overcrowded or scary, it tells us something else. In this dream, the basement is large and open, perhaps indicating spaciousness or the absence of categories or clutter within the young dreamer's subconscious.

But there *is* something in the basement, in the middle of the room— a large white dog lying atop a pillow bed. Clearly, it is the dog that is of importance here, the center of it all. That the dog is big conveys it is something sizable, important, substantial.

That the dog is white holds yet another layer of meaning. White is a color of purity, peace, simplicity or innocence, new beginnings, or even the presence of light. White animals are often rare, and almost always significant in mythology and legend. They are linked to the spirit realm—not hard to see as white is also the color of ghosts and spirits. Sometimes white animals are feared—or revered (often because they are feared). In ancient legends, a white animal is often an intermediary or guide, a being who leads humans to their destiny.

As basic dream symbols, dogs may indicate loyalty, protection, friendship, faithfulness. In this dream, the dog is friendly and relaxed, lying upon a pillow bed—suggesting rest, comfort, cushioning support, or even sleep and dreaming. The dog is welcoming and the dreamer freely approaches the dog to lie down with her upon the pillow bed, head near belly.

This placement is specific and reveals how the dreamer views the dog as openhearted, trustworthy. Perhaps the pairing of head to belly suggests the coming together of thought to feeling. Or perhaps it hints at how humans sense primarily with their brain and animals with their gut instinct. If we were so inclined, we could also look at chakras here, or energetic aspects of the body, and ask why one is brought in touch with the other.

The cohesion of symbols about the great white female dog suggests she is a protector, one who both welcomes and guards the foundation of the dreamer's inner world. Indeed, the dreamer feels comfortable enough to close her eyes. When she opens them, there is the sudden appearance of two additional dogs.

What is this bit of magic? Do the two additional dogs appear so as to emphasize "dog" in the dream? Why are they there? As I play with dream symbology, it is at this point I notice the motif of pairings and groupings that has been apparent in the dream all along. And here we have yet another way to explore our dreams—and another reason why it's so helpful to employ a variety of perspectives. As we investigate a dream element by element, we often observe deeper aspects we didn't notice on first reading the dream. Thus we are offered another path, another avenue to explore.

Just for fun, let's look at numbers in this dream since we now notice them. Two, for example, is a significant echo that reflects something about the dreamer, who is aged two and probably just learning her numbers. Returning to the beginning of the dream, we see a trinity: mother, father, child. Three is often a magical number; here it represents a complete family unit. Then we see two parents and two neighbors—a double pair, suggesting partnership, marriage, the duality of male and female. The formation of this double pairing, however, now puts the dreamer alone, the odd one out of this new grouping of five. As the two pairs move into the living room, the "one" is sent away, downward, to the basement. Is she being abased?

Interestingly, it's in the basement that the dreamer encounters another version of one—the dog. But notice how the dog reflects an entirely different aspect of one; not the odd one out but the central figure—the *one* who commands attention. Here we see how "one" can stand for autonomy and leadership; an older, more mature, confident one; one who is self-contained. If we consider the dream a rite of passage, this image of the self-contained one may foreshadow the dreamer's quest for autonomy.

When the dreamer lies beside the dog, there are two. The dreamer closes her eyes and when she opens them sees another set of two. A second instance of double pairing! But in this case, the pair of dogs are not mates (as with the parents and neighbor adults) but siblings. The two dogs are smaller, younger, more like the dreamer. In this group of four, we have a sense of mother dog and three "pups," or children. The four lie in a warm, comfortable, safe huddle. The dreamer is no longer the odd one out, but part of a family group.

Then the parents call from halfway down the basement stairs. Why halfway down? What has been halved? Have the parents lost some power or ability so they cannot fully descend? Or perhaps the dreamer has increased in some way from her time in the basement—after all, she was one alone on descending and now is part of four.

Four is three dogs plus the dreamer; four is two parents and two neighbors. One group rests in the basement, one group comes partway down. Interesting how the directional focus is no longer about the one being sent away but about the adults coming to the basement. Some subtle power has shifted.

To end, the mother comes down the stairs to take the child home (mother and child form yet another pairing). The newly formed groups dissolve and return to normal: the dogs remain in the basement; the childless neighbors stay in their home; the mother, father, and child go home. The numbers rebalance into their original format.

MANY PATHS

Again, there are many ways to interpret, many ways to follow threads of meaning in the mystery of a dream. It is up to the dreamer to sense at deeper levels what fits in her life. Further, what the dream speaks to at one time may change in another. A dream remembered is often a dream changed. And a dream remembered from childhood may age along with us, revealing hidden aspects of itself as we mature.

To open a conversation with our dreams, and to keep the conversation alive and relevant, we must be flexible. We must allow for contradiction and paradox. We must welcome a variety of paths to interpretation and multiple levels of meaning. Thus we start to ask ourselves all sorts of wild questions as a means of inviting input from different angles and directions. For example, we might consider another perspective—not from the dreamer but from the dog's point of view. What does the dog want of the child? Why does the big white dog smile at the dreamer and invite her to rest beside her? Why does the dog visit the dream? Who is the big white dog, really?

While writing this book I spent a good amount of time reviewing a large stack of old dream journals. Obviously, I did not record this dream when I was two, but the significance of the dream has stayed with me. I found I had written about it numerous times, in different journals, as if trying to recall it at different stages of my life. One description of the big white dog read, "She has alert black eyes; small, rounded ears atop her head; a long, squarish snout with a large black nose."

The more I tried to recall exactly what the dogs in the basement looked like, the less doglike they seemed. Round black eyes, curved ears atop the head, a long, square snout—could this dog be a forerunner of the great white bear?

I've often felt that bears and dogs share a common resemblance. Their shape, their walk, the compact way they move, the manner in which they sniff the earth and shake water from their bodies. Not all dogs and bears are similar of course, but in my mind there is an energetic link between Bear and Dog.

This observation has some basis in our ancient past. Before any of the eight species of modern bear who now walk our planet, before even the great cave bear from which all of these species evolved, there was *Ursavus elmensis,* the dawn bear. Short legged and well furred, she was about the size of a terrier, with characteristics that were a blend of modern dog and bear.

When I review the history of my dreams, I notice a recurring pattern in which dogs precede bears. Before the polar bear dreams there was the dog called Little High Top. And only when I remember Little High Top does the professor in the airplane hand me the invitation to dream with polar bears.

As I look back, I see the big white dog in the basement. She is watching, smiling, welcoming me to the pillow bed of dreams. Great white dog and dream guide, she is a forebear—and perhaps instigator—of all that happens next.

2

The Bear in the Closet

I'm five years old, just starting kindergarten. One autumn night in my bedroom, snuggled under the covers, I dream.

I hear a rumbling in the closet and sit up in bed. Even though it is nighttime, I can see in the dark. Everything in my room shimmers with outlines of pale white light. Fascinated, I wiggle my fingers in front of me to watch how they glimmer around the edges. Then a voice inside my head tells me that if I open the closet door I can learn how to fly.

I am a little frightened, but excited too. Of all the superpowers, the one I want most is to fly. I get out of bed, walk to the closet, and open the door. Out comes a big white bear. He talks to me in a friendly way, telling me things in that manner of the dream—not with spoken words but as a voice inside my head. We begin to walk around the edges of my room. Even though my dresser and bed are usually pushed against the wall, they are moved inward and there is a path for us, close to the wall.

The bear shows me a special way to move: sway the top of your body side to side and stretch out your legs like they are made of rubber. He also shows me how to place my feet on the floor as we walk. It is confusing at first, because he has four feet and I have two, but the faster we walk the

easier it becomes. Side by side, we circle the room, fast and smooth, until
it feels like we are gliding.

   There are invisible paths in the room. You only see them when you
move in just the right way. One looks like a ramp that leads to the ceiling.
We follow it up, out of the room, into the sky. Now I look down on the top
of my house and the roofs of all the houses on our block. We are flying!

   Then we are at the bear's home. The dark sky sparkles with stars,
and the snow and ice shine silvery white. We cross a frozen river and climb
a snowy mound. At the top the bear tells me his name. The black night
lightens, and the snow and ice turn pink.

I only vaguely remembered the dream on waking. Mostly, I remembered the good feeling of the dream. I probably could not have said, "I dreamed of a bear who taught me how to fly," but I knew that some secret process was happening, that something had been changed.

I dreamed the same dream many times that year. Each time it began with me waking in bed and recalling the bear in the closet from the dreams before. This seemed perfectly natural, and I became adept at running with the bear around my room, gliding up through the ceiling and into the sky. It was always night when we landed in the bear's home, but I could see in the same shimmery way I could in my bedroom. I was fascinated by the crisp sparkle of the air and the way we walked over the snow mound to watch the snow and ice turn pink. On waking, I typically forgot. Only while re-dreaming the dream did my dream self remember having been there before.

Throughout kindergarten, my favorite activity was painting. We took turns at the wooden easels set up in the far corner of the room. Our teacher tacked up large sheets of paper and gave us Dixie cups half-filled with paint: red, yellow, blue, white, and black. We were learning how to combine colors, and I discovered how to mix a bit of red with white to make pink. I enjoyed making dabs of falling pink snow, pink snow hills, and pink snowmen. One day my teacher commented that I must like the color pink. It struck me strange because my favorite color was blue. I looked at my classmates' easels with their paintings of square black houses, orange-leafed trees, and smiling yellow suns. And me— with all this pink snow.

Before the end of the school year, the bear was gone. I stopped painting pink snow. In first grade, we no longer had easels; we sat at desks and learned to read and write. Years passed, and although I continued to dream about a voice or presence in the closet who offered to teach me things (sometimes, to fly), I did not recall the bear. In fact, I would not remember this set of dreams for many decades. It was as if someone had neatly packed up the dreams and tucked them away, out of sight, perhaps for safekeeping. The bear was back in the closet.

For a child, meeting a friendly bear who teaches you how to fly out of your room seems a fun dream. Although it is mostly forgotten in the morning, part of the dream spills into waking life via dabs of paint. This is how an image from a dream can become a marker, a potent, personalized reminder we may not be aware of until much later in life. For me, the image of pink snow was a time-released key. When I once again saw the pink snow—in a particular way, at a particular time—it unlocked my memory and reopened the forgotten packet of dreams.

WHAT DOES IT MEAN?

Unlike the looped movement into and back from the basement of the dream in chapter 1, this dream is about moving *out.* The dreamer gets out of bed, the bear comes out of the closet, the two run around the room to fly out of the house and out of the neighborhood. In many ways, the dream is also about moving out of the ordinary. The dreamer can see in the dark. She can hear and converse without spoken words. She learns special movements that allow her to glide around the room and fly through the ceiling. Is the dream a training ground, showing the dreamer particular ways of sensing and moving out of conventional reality?

The catalyst is the bear. The bear makes the sound in the closet, waking the dreamer and teaching her the special movements that allow her to see invisible ramps and fly out of the house. There's something oddly fitting about a bear in a closet. The closet is where we hang our clothes, the costumes that cover our bare selves. But a closet also suits a bear. The dark enclosure is reminiscent of a cave where a bear might sleep. Certainly, the dream closet is also a cave of the psyche.

We store things in a closet—it is where we put objects away, out of sight. The closet may hold forgotten treasures or perhaps private wishes. It's a place of mystery. Children know that monsters can live in the closet. There's something curious about this little room within the bedroom, this small box within a box. It is a secret place where we can hide. But so, too, can the closet hide things from us. A closet holds surprises—the unknown, forgotten, or unexpected.

Before the dreamer can find out what is calling from her closet, she must pass a test. This takes the shape of a deal: open the closet door and you can learn to fly. The enticement is high—of all the superpowers, this is the one most desired. But superpowers don't come without a cost. To reap the reward, the dreamer must first do what many dreamers are called to do before the adventure can progress: face one's fear. The dreamer must choose to get out of bed, move beyond her fear, and open the door to her closet.

Of the three special talents in the dream (seeing in the dark, hearing without words, flying), the first two are givens. The dreamer simply sees and hears in this way. The movements required to learn to fly, however, must be learned. That makes me curious.

What do we make of specialized movements taught by a bear: swaying of the upper body, stretching of the legs like rubber, and special placement of feet upon the ground? (Such movements are actually very bearlike. Bears are one of the few mammals that, like humans, walk on the soles of their feet, with heel and pad upon the ground.) The teaching requires the dreamer to shift her body, to move in a particular way in order to transform. But it's not just the dreamer who does this. The bear and the dreamer circle the perimeter of the bedroom together. The movement joins them, synchronizes them, puts them in accord. The motions are done in tandem—bear and dreamer walk together, circling the room.

There always seems to be a touch of ritual in circumambulation. For the most part, we humans circle things to make them holy (i.e., we attempt to transform them by our actions), or we circle them because they are holy (and we hope to be transformed in the process). What is circled here—the bedroom, the dreamer's personal place of play and sleep and dreams—is being transformed, as are the bear and dreamer through the action.

Although it's not specifically mentioned in the dream, I remember circling the room many times—six or seven perhaps. I also recall that the circling was done counterclockwise. Is this a hint about going back in time? Because this dream was forgotten for several decades and then recalled, does it hold a sign of time travel, some element that hints at a return to the dream? Perhaps the counterclockwise motion sets something in the dream, just as we might set a timer to go off at a certain hour in the future, thus enabling the dreamer to retrieve it at a later date.

Circling the room in this particular way also creates an opening: invisible paths become visible, and a ramp provides a launching pad to move out of the room. The dreamer's world clarifies and expands. Movement with the bear allows an opening to appear.

And what of the bear's world? A land of silvery snow and ice that shines in the dark. It's night, a time of mystery and sleep, but the shimmery light is noticed for a second time in the dream. The dark sparkle of night hints again at a puzzle, the way light can also be present in darkness, just as it was in the opening of the dream. A second transformation is at play here, and the unfolding is subtle but telling: the bear and the dreamer walk over the snowy mound, the bear reveals his name, the night lets go, the snow and ice turn pink.

To be told a secret name in a dream is no small event. Notice how the bear tells the dreamer at a liminal time, just as night yields to day, the dark sparkle fading in the pink glow of early-morning sun. Although my instincts felt something important here, it took several readings of the dream to finally understand—the bear was telling me his name and showing me *mine*.

As night lets go, the dawn arrives. In this case, the color pink signals awakening. As I thought about the dream, I wondered whether this was what I was attempting to do in kindergarten so long ago in all those paintings. Was the pink snow a visual signature of my name? Is this what the dream was showing me—a way out of myself to find myself? Was the bear offering me one answer to the question that so many dreamers ask: Who am I?

As the young dreamer, it was my choice to open the closet door or not. By doing so, I let the bear out of my closet. Is there a similar choice involved in remembering dreams we have forgotten? Is there some test we need to pass, some fear to face, before we can open a door to recalling certain dream memories?

The dreams stayed hidden from my conscious awareness for almost five decades. Looking back, I wonder if the dreams were sown as seeds, not designed to sprout until a later time. Perhaps the same dream was dreamed numerous times for the same reason we scatter so many seeds in a garden—so that at least some will germinate. Did the dream contain clues to a possible future that may or may not bloom later? If I hadn't moved to Alaska, if I hadn't later met the dream bear, would I have recalled these dreams? Or even dreamed them?

Then again, perhaps the dream was designed to trigger certain experiences in my life, to say yes to certain opportunities, and to unfold only under the correct set of circumstances many decades later. Perhaps it is true, as Rilke says, that "the future enters us in order to be transformed in us, long before it happens."[1]

I have no doubt that my dreams interact, that they are part of a larger network that exists beyond the framework of our ordinary world. However, I am often amazed at how my dreams play with one another, connecting motifs, symbols, and messages, seemingly weaving ever more intricate patterns along the way. It is interesting to note, for example, how the color pink appeared in the dream of remembering Little High Top. It was only after looking out the airplane window and seeing the pink-gold color of the clouds (rippled and fluffy, not unlike pink snow) that I remembered and became lucid within that dream. Further, it was only because of this ability to recall the dream that the professor was then able to offer me the invitation.

I find it revealing to note the ways our dreams can occur and then hide, waiting for the perfect time to unfold consciously. Some dreams we may never remember. Others will only open later, when we are ready, when the time is right. Perhaps this dream was a visitation from an animal protector that was put "in the closet" until a future time when it was needed.

Did I choose to remember the bear? Or did the bear choose to awaken his memory in me?

REMEMBERING

Remembering this group of childhood dreams happened unexpectedly. I had not yet dreamed of Little High Top, nor of polar bears, and had only recently moved to Alaska.

It was early evening in late fall. The house was quiet and I was alone, sitting on the floor in the downstairs den (a symbolically appropriate location!) with a box of dream journals that I was paging through and arranging in chronological order. As I took a break from reading, I glanced out the glass door to the backyard. Snowflakes were falling and the light was shifting quickly, as it does in late-autumn Alaska. Calm and relaxed, I felt my vision guided upward, to the distant mountains.

Just then a billowy swell of light, pink and golden, spilled over the mountaintops. I watched it course down the mountainsides, across the inlet, up and over the bluff, flooding the thin layer of snow in our backyard. There was an intensity to the hue as it infused the air, filtering through snow crystals so that it seemed each falling flake was lit from within.

Pink snow! The light—a living thing, glowing radiantly—awakened something within me.

The dreams came back as easily as the pink light flowed down the mountains to meet my eyes. Like a gentle wave, the memories washed through me: hearing a noise from the closet, sitting up in bed, wiggling my fingers, watching their shimmery glow, getting out of bed, opening the closet door, circling my bedroom beside the big white bear, flying out of the ceiling and into the sky, arriving at the bear's icy home, climbing past a snow mound, watching the dark night transform to early-morning pink.

A wormhole opened inside my brain as I traveled back in time and space to my childhood bedroom. I felt the feelings and knew the thoughts that were held by my younger self. I woke up inside the dream, again, and knew myself in a new way. There was nothing fuzzy in the experience; rather, a sharp clarity in recall. It is amazing how quickly we can travel back into ourselves, into the fullness of our memories and dreams! How shocking to so vividly remember something we once knew or experienced but then forgot.

Several days later, while cleaning my closet (an obvious clue only in retrospect), I found an old box of artwork and school papers my parents had saved for me. I spent a few minutes paging through essays and poems from high school, along with reports and illustrated booklets from grade school. I had other work to do but I kept pulling the items out, layer by layer, fascinated by this personal archaeological dig. Near the bottom were some large, thin sheets of folded paper. I opened one and gazed upon a painting from long ago—a smiling girl in a white landscape surrounded by round pink hills and dabs of falling pink snow.

3
Face to Face

After the childhood dreams of flying with the white bear were forgotten, stored away in the closet of my psyche, I no longer dreamed of bears. Plenty of other animals showed up in my dreamworld over the years, but not bears. Then, on the eve of my fortieth birthday, I asked for a dream that would show me the direction of this new decade in my life. I was excited to turn forty and felt the stirrings of something dramatic. That night, an answer came from the dreamworld.

> I leave my house and turn left to walk down the street. It is late at night and everyone is asleep, all the houses dark and quiet. I feel a little thrill at being out alone. The moon shines bright and I can easily see where I am going. Passing the last house on the corner, I stand at the end of the street, at the far edge of the neighborhood.
>
> Sensing a presence, I turn left. A black bear stands upright at the edge of the forest, watching me. We remain still, frozen in the moment, looking at each other. I am alarmed, yet fascinated too. If he approaches, will I run? If I stand my ground, will he leave? What does he want?

I felt disappointment on waking. None of my questions were answered. Not knowing what would happen with the bear was like leaving a good mystery just as the secret is about to be revealed. Beyond the disappointment, however, I felt something unsettling.

I had asked for a dream but wasn't truly happy with what came. Let's be honest. I wanted a big, fancy, red-ribboned, ego-aggrandizing present of a dream for my birthday. Instead, I got a black bear who stared at me. It is a good reminder: if you're going to ask questions of your dreams, be sure you are willing to accept—and honor—the answers.

One reason we don't like certain dreams is because they show us something we don't want to see. I resisted this dream because I didn't want to know what was unsettling, why the bear was there, or what it meant that we stood so long looking at each other. Black bears felt unfamiliar to me; plus, there was the unanswered question of what would happen next.

So, what do we do with a dream that makes us feel uncomfortable? If we expect to develop a relationship with our dreaming world, the answer is clear: we engage it, pursue it, keep digging. Such dreams generally mean we're on the brink of opening to something deep and powerful.

Although I knew this intellectually, I felt uneasy. On the surface, the dream seemed small and uneventful. I could summarize it in one sentence: I walk down the street in the middle of the night, see a bear at the edge of the forest, and we stare at each other. My impatience with the dream—and ongoing desire to diminish it—suggested it probably held much more than I wanted to know.

WHAT DOES IT MEAN?

If you are unsure what a dream may be telling you, consider drawing it. This is an easy way to gain a different perspective. Following this advice, I drew a map of my house and neighborhood. I sketched our driveway and street and the path I followed to the end of the block. At that time there was a forest at the end of the neighborhood. I marked the bear's presence at the edge of the forest with an *X* and put another

X where my dream self stood, at the edge of the houses. Then I laughed. There on the map, it was all so clear; our meeting occurred at the border of our respective neighborhoods. The bear came out of the forest, the dreamer came out of her house, and there they met in the liminal no-bear-nor-woman's-land in between. The dream revealed a meeting of two worlds!

The only direction mentioned in the dream is left. As the dreamer leaves her house, she turns left. At the end of the neighborhood, she turns left again, this time to face the bear. A turn to the left makes me think about the right and left sides of the body, which are controlled by the opposite sides of the brain. To be left-brained is to be rational, logical, analytical; for most people this corresponds to the right side of the body. To be right-brained is to use intuition, instinct, and holistic views; this corresponds to the left side of the body. A left turn of the body may thus indicate a turn to one's instincts, to intuition, to the unconscious, or perhaps to the creative, holistic associations of the dreamworld. (It was once believed the devil stood on one's left side, nudging us over to the shadow world.) When the dreamer turns to her left, she faces the bear. And there he stands: Animal teacher? Guardian of the forest? Dark-furred representative of the wild nature of the psyche?

As a symbolic animal guide, Bear's teaching is vast. It can include introspection, discernment, healing, transformation, solitude, wisdom, visionary dreams, the ability to mediate between the living and the dead, and awakening the unconscious. How do we know which aspect of Bear (or any animal) is appearing to us? How do we find the particular brand of medicine our dream animal is offering? To begin, we might ask some basic questions: What is the bear doing in the dream? Is there anything special or unusual going on? How is the bear standing, sitting, acting, moving?

In this dream, the bear is alert and observant, watching the dreamer as she approaches. (A subtle reminder, perhaps, that the unconscious is already many steps ahead of us.) The bear stands upright. Bears were often revered in ancient times for precisely this reason: they can stand

and walk on two legs, like humans. The connection between bear and human is old and deep. Some researchers cite Paleolithic origins in bear ceremonialism, as our distant Stone Age ancestors honored bear carcasses and skulls with decorations. In different parts of the world, humans created taboos and elaborate rituals for hunting and eating bear. In some cultures bears were so revered they were considered gods. Many Native cultures intuitively knew that Bear was a powerful spirit. Thus, they reasoned, one should treat a bear with utmost respect, both in life and death. Because bear spirits can hear your words, it is not wise to speak ill of them, for subsequent events can go terribly wrong. Even still there is a sensed kinship between bears and humans in many cultures, as in the Native American expressions of honor, Grandfather Bear and Grandmother Bear.

Bears stand upright to gain a better view of their surrounding terrain and what lies ahead. This reveals the inquisitive, adaptable side of black bears. In the dream, the bear's posture may indicate a look to the future, especially as it reflects the dreamer's invoked question, What lies ahead for me?

The black bear is the smallest of Alaskan bears. In addition to standing upright like humans, their footprints reveal the full length of their soles touching the ground, as do ours. (This trait is uncommon among mammals, making it an intriguing link that unites bears and humans.) Another unique quality about black bears is that they are excellent tree climbers. But this dream bear is on the ground. It stands on its own two feet—advice perhaps to stand one's ground or step in to one's personal power?

We might also find clues to the nature of this dream bear through its coloring. Black can symbolize what is unknown or unconscious: death, darkness, mystery, fear. In this sense, the black bear may be calling the dreamer to a deeper understanding of what is unknown or hidden from her conscious self.

Although these are very simple, basic overviews of the dream, even this initial dip into the pool of symbolism can shift the gist of a one-sentence dream from *I walk down the street, see a bear at the edge of the forest, and we stare at each other* to *At the entrance to my unconscious, Bear the Guardian stands and watches me;* or *Standing at the edge of what is known in my neighborhood, I face the unknown forest of the psyche and glimpse the ancient power of Bear.*

Sometimes just a peek below the surface of a dream can change everything. It is good to meet a black bear at the entrance to your future, I decided. And yet, that disconcerting *something* about the dream still niggled at me. When I closed my eyes, I could see the bear standing upright, surveying its neighborhood, looking my way. I was waiting to see what Bear would do, but deeper contemplation offered another idea: perhaps Bear was watching to see what I would do. And this caused me to consider, what does Bear want with me?

MORE BEARS

In the next eight years, I had six more dreams in which I met a bear in the forest. The dreams were connected and followed both a pattern and a progression, yet because there was so much time between the dreams, I didn't recognize them as a series until much later.

Although I initially dreamed of black bears, later dreams involved larger brown bears and grizzlies (a subspecies of the brown bear). Looking back at the dreams now, I wonder if Bear was frustrated with me. Did it sense I couldn't (or wouldn't) understand what it was trying to convey, and so felt a need to become bigger, more dramatic and extreme? At the same time, the larger bears became ever more human-looking, sometimes wearing human clothes and making human gestures. This was just one of the interesting contradictions that infused this collection of dreams.

Although the dream stories were similar in plot and pattern, each had its unique variation. Further, a progression was occurring within the dreams as a whole. One of the first versions of this dream series goes like this.

I live in a small cabin in the woods. I have been away and, on returning home, discover there is a bear in the house. I am afraid for myself and my young daughter, who is with me. I quickly lock the bear inside the cabin. But I'm also curious, so I watch from an outside window. The bear stands on two feet, like a human. He turns to me and we look at each other. For a moment I recognize him and realize he knows me as well. But suddenly I panic and look away. I grab my daughter's hand and we run to find someone to help—someone to kill the bear.

The last dream of the series reveals more details and some significant changes in the dreamer's attitude.

I am walking through a forest and pass a huge tree that has a window in its trunk. I stop to look inside and see a large brown bear in a spacious, wood-paneled room. He is walking upright across the floor, beautifully dressed in billowy, sky-blue pants and an ornate embroidered vest. He has wire-rimmed glasses and is carrying a cup of tea. I am surprised how cozy his home seems, with its big easy chair and footstool. The bear stands casually with his cup of tea and browses through shelves of old, well-worn books. When he turns to face me, our eyes meet and a rush of affection fills the space between us. I feel so happy to see him! But just as suddenly, I remember I've called the authorities. They are coming to shoot the bear, to kill him. My heart sinks. I am horrified, beside myself, sick with fear. The bear will be killed, and there is nothing I can do.

On waking from these dreams, I felt some very keen despondency. Sometimes, in the first few seconds of awakening, I felt physical panic: heart racing, nerves twitching, stomach wrenching. In the earliest dreams, my dream self panicked and ran away, looking for someone to kill the bear. In later dreams, however, my dream self despaired with a sick fear that the bear, who hadn't hurt anyone, would be killed.

Many humans fear wild animals, and in North America bears are one of the biggest animals we fear. Indeed, bears can be dangerous. Large and immensely powerful, with sharp claws and teeth, bears can kill us. It's not only a societal fear but a cellular fear borne of evolution. Over the ages we have developed, and continue to reinforce, deeply ingrained fears about the wild in general—of which Bear is a key representative.

In contrast to the fear, however, these dreams also hold moments of wondrous connection, a sudden awakening in which the dreamer feels she genuinely knows the bear and the bear knows the dreamer. In that moment, in the center of the dream, recognition blooms and a link of deeper relationship is revealed. And yet, fear returns—though fear for a different reason: the dreamer realizes she has called the authorities to kill the bear.

Clearly, there is progression within this dream series. The dreamer's position shifts from being fearful of the bear and searching for someone to kill it, to feeling affection for the bear but fearing she cannot undo her call for its demise. Although the dream bear is not violent or even particularly scary, the dreamer attempts to engage other humans to kill the bear. To my perception, it seems that both personal avoidance as well as unconscious, collective fears are involved here.

And yet, isn't it curious that these dreams are set in the midst of bear territory? The dreamer ventures into the forest (to her cabin—an interesting clue revealing that some part of the dreamer lives in the wild, too) or walks through the wilderness. When the dreamer comes upon the bear, she locks him in her cabin, or watches him in his house within the tree. In either case, the bear is contained, separated, observed within an enclosure.

The dreamer's cabin is made of logs, and the bear's home is a tree. Further, a wood-paneled room within a tree suggests the dream makers would like us to notice these materials: wood and trees. Trees can represent many things in our dreams—growth, nourishment, shade, protection, stability, rootedness, or connection between land and sky, earth and heaven. In this dream, the tree protects and provides shelter. It also creates a boundary. The tree is a home, and something special— the bear—is held both within the wood cabin and the tree. (This motif also brings to mind the closet in which the young dreamer once found a bear, held behind a wooden door in her bedroom.)

When the dreamer and bear face each other, they *see* each other and a deeper relationship is recognized. In that moment, the dreamer is no longer fearful; in fact, she experiences a rush of warm feelings toward the bear. Something is being opened here. Something is recalled, reawakened within the forest of the dreamer's psyche, within her own sacred "tree of life." But just as quickly, this something is shut down. The dreamer allows the emotions of panic or regret to cloud the awakening clarity; she succumbs to the clutches of fear.

When I reread these dreams, I marvel at how elegantly our dream creators weave together symbols and story, how persistent they are in attempting to convey to the waking self a message. Both individually and as a group, the dreams hold tension and contradiction. The dreamer is fearful yet curious, alarmed yet fascinated. When the dreamer returns to her home in the forest, she finds a wild bear; later, when passing through the forest, she watches a bear dressed like a human in a human-like home. What is this curious inversion? Some internal friction is at work here, some churning of deeper emotions and attitudes, some force coming to light—just for a moment, but yet to be fully awakened.

No wonder the initial birthday dream evoked unsettling feelings! As the dreams progress, they reveal the dreamer's conflicting views about her relationship with the bear (and with herself). It's a repetitive pattern that seeks to be resolved.

We still don't know where these dreams will lead, however. There is no resolution, no real ending. Rather, the dreams disclose a tension, an ongoing struggle within the dreamer. Dreams like this are snapshots from the psyche, updated maps of where we are in our lives. Such dreams reflect our inner world by acting as personalized, encoded mirrors. They show us something about ourselves and the relationship between our outer and inner worlds.

In this respect, my waking disappointment with the birthday dream made another kind of sense, for to wake from a dream story before it is finished may cause us to ask, In what way am I being called to awaken?

The small black bear stands upright, curious and watchful; the brown bear in blue, billowy pants stands casually, self-possessed, at home within his tree of life. Teacher, ally, powerful dreamtime advisor, Bear urges us to look inside ourselves when we need help. As I wrote in *Animal Teachings,* "Bear knows that in the calm silence of our deepest being, we can see and hear clearly. Alert and aware in the dreamworld, we will find our answers."[1]

Bear is an appropriate symbol for both personal and cultural awakening. Author Ted Andrews remarks, "Bear medicine can teach you to go deep within so that you can make your choices and decisions from a position of power."[2] The question is, are we ready to step in to our power? Are we ready to access what some dreamers and mythic explorers call the "world behind the world"? Are we willing to bring the creative, dormant knowledge held in our unconscious into the open, into consciousness, into our everyday lives?

No wonder such a muddled mixture of fear and fascination accompanies so many human transitions! The outcome of our future lies in our hands, our minds, our hearts, our souls—just as it has always been. Are we ready to wake from the dream?

If the answer is yes, then how? And when? And at what cost? For more answers, we dream on . . .

4
The Power That Hunts Us

We sometimes don't know the significance of a dream until much later. Or perhaps we *feel* it, but don't have the means to fully understand or express it until a more distant time. Often we need the dream to ripen, to allow its message to unfold inside of us, to point us in the right direction, or to remind us what we already know.

It was only after the dream of meeting the professor on the airplane, after he handed me the invitation to dream with polar bears, and after I began walking beside a polar bear in an Arctic dreamscape that it occurred to me to search for bear motifs in my journals. This was a time-consuming but compelling task. Although the previous three chapters describe an orderly progression of dreams, my recall and subsequent discovery of connections within and between the dreams would not have been possible without referring to the stack of journals I've kept since age twelve.

A REVIEW

Even before consulting the journals, I knew my earliest dream—that of the big white dog in the basement—was the start of it all. Although no bears were apparent in the dream, it *felt* like a bear dream. As I skimmed through decades of journal entries, notes, and sketches, I discovered that I had written about this dream many times during my life. Viewing it from different vantage points, I began to unlock its deeper significance. The dream became a personal myth, my relationship with it changed, and I even came to wonder if that dog was not, in fact, a bear.

Next in chronology were the dreams of the white bear in the closet who taught me to fly. He took me to his icy world and whispered his name into my ear. This group of dreams was magical and childlike, involving flight and light and transformation. Magical, too, was the way the dreams disappeared from my consciousness. Stowed away on a back shelf in the closet of my psyche, they stayed hidden for more than four decades, until a vision of pink snow triggered recall.

The third set of bear dreams was initiated by an incubated dream borne of a desire to preview my life's direction at age forty. The dark bear standing at the edge of the forest was a forebear of sorts, ushering in a series of dreams that triggered wonder and fascination, as well as frustration and fear. The common pattern of encountering a bear in a forest connected six more dreams, yet they were spread out over eight years. Because so much time passed between the dreams, it was only in rereading them that I recognized their common theme. I thought of the dream professor as I paged through these years in my journals, aware that without his invitation I would likely not be searching for bears in the first place—nor realize these dreams were actually a series! It's fascinating how a character in a dream can nudge us to backtrack and connect the dots, and how, by paying attention, we are so often rewarded with unexpected help, encouragement, and support.

It was soon after the bear-in-the-forest dreams ended that I dreamed of Little High Top. Like my early childhood dream of the big white dog in the basement, this was not truly a bear dream since no bear was involved. However, my lucid memory of Little High Top one year later caused a dream professor to hand me an invitation to dream with bears. *Dreaming with polar bears* was the ticket—offered and accepted—

that led to the next series of dreams of walking beside a polar bear in the Arctic. The dreams were short and sporadic and occurred for nearly a year. As noted in the introduction, these dreams felt like hard little seeds. I sensed the dreams as different from others: self-contained and seemingly impervious to my toolbox of dream techniques. And yet, as we have already observed, dreams are not isolated but often work together, blending, prompting, elaborating, and elucidating. A single dream can initiate a domino effect, triggering actions, events, and memories in other dreams in an attempt to open us from within. Fallout from one dream bombards another, activating clues, symbols, and messages across the vast dreamscape, nudging, whispering, calling us to attention. For me, this was how two "ordinary" night dreams—dreamed within a week of each other—helped to quicken my awareness and crack open the Arctic seed dreams from within.

CROSSING BOUNDARIES

The first dream was set in northern Wisconsin, in the home my husband and I lived in shortly after marrying. It was a small, old, wood-framed house that overlooked a tiny tree-rimmed lake. The house was built into a hill. From the front yard it appeared to be one level, but owing to the hill you could walk in the front door, descend the basement stairs, and come out again at ground level through the back door. At the time, we lived in the house with Barney, my old, wise canine pal, though he had passed on many years before this dream occurred. The dream was a powerful one.

Barney is barking loudly in the basement. I rush downstairs to investigate and discover he has already pushed open the back door and run outside. From the doorway, I watch him barking at a thin wire fence separating backyard from forest and lake. On the other side of the fence is a polar bear, his head low to the ground, nose to nose with Barney.

I yell at Barney to get inside, but he is persistent and keeps barking.

He squeezes past a flimsy gateway in the fence and scrambles under the bear. Nonchalantly, the bear pushes him away with his front paw, as if to toss him backward, out of the way. But one of his long claws slices into Barney's side and catches the skin. I scream as the barking suddenly stops and Barney lands in a heap behind the bear—his fur peeled back, his skin turned inside out.

Calmly, the polar bear pushes open the gate with his head and saunters toward me. I quickly shut the door and lock it, but there's a big gap in the doorjamb and I realize it won't hold for long. I run across the basement, back up the stairs, and slam shut the door at the top. There is no lock, so I stack boxes in front of the door. But I know it's useless; this will not keep the bear away.

My mother was visiting when I had this dream. I still remember how she clamped her hands over her mouth when I described the bear's claw snagging Barney's side, peeling back his skin in the momentum of the push. "That's horrible!" she exclaimed. It's true; witnessing a beloved dog turned inside out, landing in a lifeless, bloody lump, is appalling—as is the heart-pounding panic that causes you to bolt when a polar bear strolls your way. So, why did I feel so encouraged by this dream?

Our feelings about dreams can be insightful guides, alerting us to the possibility of larger views, deeper meanings, and far-reaching perspectives. Feelings that seem contrary to the surface description of a dream often present a challenge to the waking self. What to do? When events or images from a dream frighten us, will we break down with denial and avoidance, or will we break through? Are we willing to move beyond what is initially off-putting? Will we trust the truth of what we feel?

Even though my dream self was fearful and ran from the bear, my waking self felt something powerful and exciting at play. After all, a small white dog walked out of the basement of my being, and a big white bear sauntered in. Key elements in my psyche were rearranging—turning inside out, dying, renewing, transforming—and to me this felt not only appropriate but necessary. The dream was a signal to be alert to change.

Powerful and exciting too was the fact that the dream brought me back to the basement, back to the iconic white dog guardian (in this dream, portrayed by Barney) who started it all. Just as my waking self was reviewing past dreams, searching for connections and clues, the dream creators returned me to a similar setting as in my first remembered dream. A larger cycle was guiding me round.

WHAT DOES IT MEAN?

As we have explored in previous chapters, breaking down a dream into objects, actions, characters, and events allows us to consider the aspects of each with greater detail. It's helpful to write down a dream soon after waking, for the words and phrases we choose to describe a dream also hold clues. Later, we can free-associate these expressions along with ideas, images, and memories. We can let go, as if in a dream, allowing the subconscious mind to flow and play, while at the same time observing, watching for additional hints and suggestions. This is often how we discover visual and verbal puns, innuendos, signals, inklings, pointers, and signs to deeper meaning. The dreamworld is symbolically rich, vastly rewarding. Sometimes just one word or a single image can give rise to so many questions that we end up with a multiplicity of insights.

For example (and fun), let's consider the dream's opening line: *Barney is barking loudly in the basement.* This short sentence offers three significant clues: a dog (specifically being white, fluffy, old, named Barney; and symbolically representing a known guardian and protector), barking loudly (making noise, warning the dreamer, calling her to attention), in the basement (the psyche, the subconscious, a deeper perspective, the foundation of the dreamer's being). Though no longer alive in the waking world (a hint that we are going back in time or dealing with material from the dreamer's past?), the dog alerts the dreamer—*Someone's here. Something's happening. Come quick!*

We could take each one of these clues and probe deeper. For example, the noise of the bark calls the dreamer down to the basement. But why a bark? Does it signify a need to activate expression, to bark freely, to voice one's true feelings? Perhaps it is about annoyances or distractions, an auditory reflection of bothersome thoughts within the dreamer's mind. Or perhaps it evokes memory of another bark, from a dream in which a dog named Little High Top bark-coughed in unison with the dreamer.

There are many questions we can pose not only about a first line but also of background elements not initially apparent: the setting, time, or opening framework of a dream. Why, for example, do events occur in this particular house from the dreamer's past? Dreams involving a former residence may refer to significant events in our psyche's development from that stage of life. The dreamer's house was the first she inhabited with her husband soon after marriage. Perhaps this indicates that a similar type of transition or rite of passage will be presented in the dream. Then again, the dreamer recalls the house as small and old. Does this point to something she has outgrown—outdated thinking or small-minded beliefs? Do past attitudes need to be updated and renewed; does the dreamer's perspective need to evolve? Or, perhaps this house is featured because it is built into a hill, partially protected by the earth (hinting at what's underground, sheltered in the subconscious), and yet opens on two different ground levels (is the dreamer "grounded" in two different worlds?).

It can be helpful to play with our dreams like this, to allow ourselves the freedom to ask all sorts of questions, to pull any thread that catches our attention, to follow any detour or out-of-the-way diversion that beckons. We may encounter a few dead ends, of course, but sometimes the most unlikely thought leads us to the most potent insight. Trust yourself when exploring. Follow leads and intuitive nudges, consider the insights—no matter how quirky—that occur. We can *feel* when we're onto something.

MOVEMENT

Although I often play with symbols and interpretation shortly after writing down a dream, I didn't feel inclined to do so with this dream. Rather, it replayed in my mind for several days, without conscious analysis. At times, I had the intention to pause in the dream and question the bear, to ask it why it was there. But the dream did not agree to my game. Once playing in my mind, it continued without stopping, as if it needed to run the length of its duration. The dream energized me; I felt something was happening or going to happen very soon.

I understand now why this was so. The dream was about movement. Though it included pauses of movement—moments of observation from the dreamer's vantage—it was mostly about moving past boundaries. I sensed an underlying message about needing to complete something or see it through.

Looking at the structure of the dream, we may notice the obvious presence of borders and boundaries: the door to the basement, the backdoor to the lake, the wire fence with the inset gateway. Doors and fences separate and partition; they order, categorize, delineate; they keep things in and they keep things out. But this dream was about *crossing* boundaries—opening and moving through gateways, as well as closing them, attempting to stop the movement of change.

The dream also highlights the liminal space between gateways. Notice how the dreamer lingers in the open basement doorway, neither fully inside nor outside, and yet a little of both. The dream positions the dreamer in the transitional zone between categories, in that rite of passage middle space that holds possibility, as well as danger.

Interestingly, the white dog—the guardian, the one who has summoned the dreamer down—has already passed through two barriers (the door down to the basement and the basement door to the backyard) when the dreamer arrives. But he is stopped by the third: the thin wire fence separating backyard from forest and lake. (There's always an element of magic in the third; always a hint that we are nearing the most important part of the story.) Plenty of associations come to mind about this fence: it separates the yard from nature; what is tamed from what is wild; that which is private and individual (as in "our own backyard") from larger collective energies or primeval forces in the subconscious or unconscious (the forest and lake). The fence also separates dog from bear (known, loyal friend from unknown, wild animal). Dog and bear are nose to nose (a telling expression hinting at curiosity as well as olfactory intelligence), and the scene offers the dreamer a chance to observe her waking idea that bears and dogs are connected in a meaningful way.

When the dog crosses the third border, the fence, transformation occurs. What was inside the border goes out—and is dramatically turned inside out. And what was outside the border now comes in. A gateway has been broken through and opened. There's a shift of form. The old white dog is retired and the polar bear joins the dreamer in his place. Indeed, the dreamer has been summoned down into her psyche to witness this: the death of the old, the arrival of the new.

When I re-watch this dream, I see elegance in the polar bear's movements. He is not angry or trying to hurt the dog; rather, he is just a bit annoyed by the barking and so swoops back his front paw as if to push the dog away. Transformation occurs through movement, in the momentum of a push. And then, in the blink of an eye, everything has changed. Before the transformation: loud, persistent barking. After: silence and a scream.

As the transformation concludes, the bear crosses the fence and moves into the dreamer's territory (her home, her self, her soul). This causes the dreamer to panic and run. Not surprisingly, it's often our impulse to run away from big animals who move toward us (especially big animals that turn smaller animals inside out). But who, really, is the bear?

As author Robert Moss notes, the Australian Aborigines say that the big stories—"the stories worth telling and retelling, the ones in which you may find the meaning of your life—are forever stalking the right teller, sniffing and tracking like predators hunting their prey."[1] Disguised as something fierce, challenging, scary, the Big Story looks for someone—you?—to carry its deeper message to the conscious world and share with others.

I knew something important was happening with this dream. I felt the challenge, the fear—and the opportunity. If polar bears hadn't been on my mind, if I hadn't been dreaming of walking beside a polar bear quite often, it would have been a natural question to ask, Why a polar bear? But this was personal; the polar bear was not simply a symbol or archetype. Even though my dream self was frightened and ran away, it was rewarding to see this bear in the dream. I felt a deeper awareness of my dream life quickening.

In the last scene, the dreamer attempts to close the door to the bear, but there is an obvious gap in the doorway and it will not hold for long. The old ways of keeping things out will no longer work. This is echoed at the end of the dream when the dreamer runs up the stairs and slams shut the door, attempting to create a barricade with boxes (an interesting image, representing an attempt to order, store, or "box up" old memories, ideas, emotions, and ways of being). The action is an obvious attempt to keep what has entered the basement from reaching the first floor (conscious awareness), but—as the dreamer knows—this won't keep the bear away. Boundaries have been crossed. And the dreamer knows that once we let the bear out of the basement, we will never be the same.

One night, just before dozing off, the dream replayed in my mind's eye once again. I hear the bark, race down the basement stairs, witness the white dog and the white bear as they interact, feel panic as the bear looks to me, and so race back through the basement and up the stairs, slamming shut the door.

And then, in that sleepy twilight state, I pause. Instead of stacking boxes against the door, I wonder what will happen if I open the door—just a bit. I feel my fingers on the doorknob, turning. Peering into the dark basement, I sense the presence of Bear at the top of the stairs, his breath warm little puffs just beyond the crack of the door.

"What do you want?" I ask.

To find you, he replies.

5

Dancing with the Polar Bear

One last dream, one final encounter before the hard little seed dreams of walking beside a polar bear in the high Arctic will crack open, ushering in a new way of being with the bear. It begins gently.

Walking through a forest, I come to a grassy clearing with several huge stone formations. They are bright white, smooth and rounded, with human-size holes and hollows. People are walking around, kids playing on the grass. I pass through an archway in one of the stones. Coming out, I notice a grizzly bear at the edge of the forest, watching us. I freeze and tell a nearby woman that we should move away slowly. As the bear's presence becomes known, fear breaks loose and people start to run and shout. I run with them, away from the bear, into a shopping mall.

The bear follows us inside, and we run out of the mall. People shove through the door onto a white stone plaza. Most everyone gets out, but the bear is close behind. I shut the glass door and try to lock it. No one will help me. I see there's a woman still inside, the bear at her back. I look in her eyes and feel sad to betray her.

Then the bear is out—no longer a grizzly, but a polar bear. People rush around the plaza, which has large white stones similar to those in the clearing, though more angular and geometric, like tall statues of modern art. As I notice the stones so does everyone else, and we share the same thought: We can't outrun the bear, but we can freeze and pretend to be statues.

The bear moves from person to person, sniffing each of us. When he comes to me, he stands upright and I know—I am the one he is looking for. Without thinking, I leap to embrace him. Big and warm and furry, he holds me close. I realize I love him, have always loved him. We dance around the people and the statues, round and round the plaza.

I awoke from the dream on waves of happiness. The flashes of recognition I shared with the bear in previous dreams were at last brought home in physical embrace. Musing on the dream, I felt a deepening sense of connection as images, memories, and symbols from past dreams settled over me like a warm, familiar shawl. But less than an hour later, drinking coffee at the kitchen table, recording the dream in my journal, a nervous wave of fear shivered through me.

WHAT DOES IT MEAN?

We can usually feel when we're on the brink of something big. For me, such feelings are often accompanied by a mixture of elation and apprehension.

It had been nearly half a century since my dream self first opened the closet door and met the polar bear. My child self had trusted the bear—walked beside him and learned a new way of moving so as to fly up through my bedroom ceiling and visit his icy home at the top of the world. But within a year, those dream memories were packed away, the bear back in the closet.

When the bear finally reappeared decades later, he showed up as a black bear standing at the edge of my neighborhood, observing. It made me nervous, as if a challenge or test was involved. The bear was watching me—and would continue to do so for many years. Successive dreams revealed both my unease around the bear as well as curiosity. Tension was evident—a growing familiarity with the bear, knowing that something was being asked of me, juxtaposed with angst and worry.

"What do you want?" I had asked the polar bear at the top of my basement stairs only a few nights before. *To find you,* he answered.

And found me, he had! I felt my latest dream was both a summary and culmination of all the bear dreams to date. It held similar situations and symbolic connections to past dreams, as if the dream creators had been riffling through and using elements of previous dreams to create this one. The dreamer sees the grizzly watching from the edge of the forest just as the forty-year-old dreamer once saw the black bear watching her from the edge of her neighborhood. The dreamer dances loopy circles around the plaza just as the child dreamer once glided around her bedroom.

Unlike the dream from chapter 4, there are no fences or borders in this dream. There is a door, however—the glass door in the mall. As the dreamer exits she tries to lock it, to keep the bear inside. I felt at once this was a nod to all the dreams in the forest, a memory of the many times my dream self tried to keep the bear locked inside a cabin or a tree (or, as in the previous dream, to prevent the bear from coming inside my home).

The people run into the mall to get away from the bear, and then out again to escape the bear. Inside, outside—the dreamer can't get away from the bear. But a woman is left inside. The dreamer looks into her eyes and feels sad to betray her. An interesting word, *betray*—the etymological roots remind us that to betray is to hand over, to give up, to reveal involuntarily. Is the woman locked in the mall with the bear at her back a reflection of the dreamer looking through the glass door? Or perhaps she is a lost self, forgotten in some part of the dreamer's psyche. What has been revealed involuntarily? That some part of the dreamer is still locked away, the bear breathing down her back? And what is a bear doing in a mall? Do the people run away because they fear the bear will maul them?

There are many such questions we could tease from this dream, more comparisons easily discovered. But this dream announces from the start that something significant has changed. No longer is the dreamer meeting the bear in the forest, but emerging from that subconscious dreamworld to a clearing—an open space of clarity.

And then—those great, white, human-size stone statues! Like a charm, a special key, a reminder of their importance, three times the dreamer encounters some version of the white stone: first in the clearing—smooth and rounded, with human holes and hollows; later in the plaza—tall geometric statues evoking modern art; and (a bit less evident, though plain to see) as the foundational stone of the plaza itself.

As dream symbols, large stones suggest solidity, strength, permanence. Stone may signify something hard or unyielding; though in this dream, stone is revealed artistically as sculpture and foundation for sacred space. Indeed, stones often hold a sense of the sacred, of tradition, and magic. This is not a dream about stoning (retribution) or being stoned (altering one's consciousness via hallucinogens) but about moving through and acting like stone, perhaps communing with the nature of stone—white stone in particular. In some ancient traditions, a white stone equals acquittal, goodness, purity, and enlightenment. In this dream, white stone evokes strength, fortitude, stability.

When a polar bear meanders through your dream, images of irregularly shaped white stones (both rounded and geometric) and a white plaza may understandably bring the Arctic to mind. Imagine the white stones as snowy land and ice, the varied shapes of icebergs and ice formations—some rounded smooth, others sharp and angular. Perhaps the dreamer's white stone statues represent frozen thoughts and feelings?

The dreamer "freezes" twice in the dream—in the beginning when she sees the grizzly standing at the edge of the forest, and later when sharing a group thought that escaping the bear might be achieved by freezing like a statue. While this ploy doesn't fool the bear from its quest to find what it is looking for, it does allow time for the dreamer to deepen. It's an interesting twist on the notion of being frozen. In some dreams, we might be frozen with fear, paralyzed into inaction. But in this dream freezing like a statue requires the dreamer to stay still, to be present in the scene, and ultimately to face her fear. When at last the dreamer sees that the bear is looking for her, recognition occurs. A spark of deeper knowing activates the leap of embrace—the dreamer no longer frozen and no longer in fear.

THE BIG STORY

Embracing the polar bear seemed to me a spiral back to the sense of belonging I experienced in earlier dreams—communing with the big white dog, gliding around my bedroom with the big white bear. I felt my bear dreams coming together, as if each one was a jigsaw piece of a much larger picture.

It would only be a week until the Arctic dream came again, when all that had been held and frozen in my dream psyche would crackle open as I turn my head, reach out my hand, look at the bear, and *know*. We would see each other in a different way, as if for the first time, lucid and aware, and a new path would arise.

Many peoples throughout different periods of history have embraced dreaming as a vehicle to deeper connection with self and soul. Dreams may convey messages from the divine, whispers from our own subconscious, visits from alternate selves. The inner world calls to us, offering suggestion and encouragement. Sometimes our job is not simply to decode but to integrate—to bring lost or forgotten pieces of ourselves back into the light, to become whole.

Once we open to our dreams, they open to us. We become privy to the secret gateways that swing open between dreams and waking life, between our imagination and our projected perceptions upon the world. Meaning is much more multilayered than our ordinary consciousness assumes. Symbols and signs are everywhere, always.

When the Big Story is hunting us, it may test us—many times perhaps, challenging us to determine if we are ready. When we get closer to what we really want (and to what wants us), we're asked to be more fully present, more engaged with who we really are. The Big Story challenges us to wake up. And this can be both exciting and frightening.

We dissect dreams in order to understand. We find meaning in our projections upon the world, and we desperately crave something that we've so long forgotten: to know who we really are. Sometimes the questions are more important than the answers. For to ask a good question is to begin to know.

What do our dreams want from us? The deeper realization that I knew and loved the polar bear brought the import of the dream professor's question to mind. Is Little High Top real? Is the polar bear real? As James Hillman notes in *Dream Animals,* "All this brilliance in digging out the meaning of animal presences in human dreams never lets the animals present themselves as they are."[1]

What happens next is a beginning, an exploration of what it means to dream *with* an animal rather than about one. To do that, we will stop looking at dreams about bears, and begin to see another perspective as we walk alongside the polar bear.

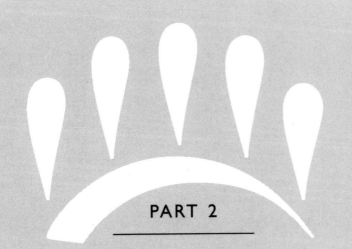

PART 2

The Meeting Place

Always relationship!

THE POLAR BEAR COUNCIL

6
Arctic Dreamers

The dreams of walking beside the polar bear in the high Arctic were short and simple. Always we were moving—one foot, one paw, in front of the other—calm, deliberate, steady. Different dreams featured different landscapes: open snow plains, jagged ice fields, frozen ocean. There were different colors as well: whites and blues and foggy grays; shimmering bands of pink, purple, orange, and red in the sun's low glow; slick silver ice, metallic with moonlight; black heavens with milky star shine; and the undulating aurora—yellow, green, and neon blue.

Why the Arctic, I sometimes wondered. Set beside the obvious fact that this is where we find polar bears, it seemed a silly question. But look again, listen; there is an open, clean, uncluttered quality about the Arctic. There is snow and ice, water and wind, air and light—a marked absence of human diversions.

I didn't think in the dreams. There were no questions or wonderings. Rather, the rhythmic walking settled me into being. I sensed light and landscape interacting, an intimacy of shapes and colors I had never noticed. There was a complex yet simple relationship between the elements. It wasn't something I thought, but something I felt—everything connected, integral, essential.

Walking was a means of locating a deeper place of connection, both in myself and in the dreamscape. And the Arctic was a perfect setting.

As noted, these dreams continued for about a year. I called them seed dreams; perhaps I sensed that something was being sowed. I realized I was becoming entrained as well. The repetition of movement, precise and methodical, reminded me of walking beside the polar bear around my bedroom as a child. I remembered the special way of moving that allowed me to sync with the bear, to see the invisible ramps that led up out of my bedroom into the dark sky, to fly to the polar bear's home.

Walking is an ancient form of meditation, a powerful means to sink into self. (The Polar Bear people are masters of this, able not only to dream while walking but also to use walking as a means of consciously entering a dream.) I started to *feel* throughout my body. I could sense the energetic vibration of land and snow, ice and water beneath my feet. It flowed through my soles, up my legs and spine, into my arms and fingers. It was a year of necessary training, this ongoing meditation of movement, for it allowed me to attune to the finer, subtle energies of shared dreaming. By deepening movement, I was learning to deepen myself, to open my consciousness in more expansive ways.

It took time. The professor's invitation to dream with polar bears initiated the seed dreams, and my curiosity with these dreams initiated a review of past bear dreams, and this action initiated two additional dreams that quickened my opening, helping to crack open the seed dreams from within. And while this ordered portrayal of one thing leading to another is true, it is not the full story. At deeper levels, the dreams were connected more like webs than timelines. They touched each other, influencing and encouraging, allowing awakening to occur in precisely the right moment. For me, the dreams were an ongoing training ground, a collection of independent yet interrelated challenges that revealed my stage of readiness for the bears, for the Big Story, and for all that followed.

Indeed, I now think those tough little seed dreams were impervious to my attempts at interpretation for very good reason. Yet at the time this was frustrating. Eventually, I learned to let go of my need to understand in the waking world and simply experienced the dreams. And then, at last, came the seed dream that bloomed into awakening. Although this dream has already been described in the introduction of this book, it is recounted here again because it was such a milestone in my dream relationship with the polar bear.

It is night and I am walking beside the polar bear across a wide, flat, silvery expanse of snow. The air is crystalline, sharp and clear. I notice a rhythm in our walk, something distinct and familiar. Slowly, I come to realize that I have been here before; this is a dream. I have dreamed this dream before—I am dreaming now. The recognition is both obvious and amusing. Laughing, I reach out to touch the bear's shoulder and he turns his great white head to me. I realize I am quite calm, not overly excited as I usually am in lucid dreams. For a moment I want to ask the bear, Why are we here? What are we doing? But my awareness is now also within the bear. He is looking at me, into me, and I see myself through his eyes. He remembers me; he has seen me before, in his dreams. Then I realize that not only am I dreaming but he is dreaming, too. In fact, we are both awake, lucid and aware, within each other's dream.

The awareness that I was dreaming, that the bear was dreaming, and that we were both lucid and *seeing* each other inside a joined dream was the beginning of a remarkable collaboration. It led to more dreams, filled with dialogues and adventures, not only with that unique polar bear dreamer, but with groups of bears involved with specialized dream teachings that, they said, were part of planetary evolution.

Part 1 was a personal sharing of dreams—an exploration of my history of dreaming about bears, how bear symbology evolved in my dreamworld, and how my projected fears and fascinations with bears changed over the years. Part 2 takes us to a shared dreamscape. In this section, we shift from symbolic dream interpretations to specific dreamworld locales—meeting places that allow two or more lucid dreamers to converse within a shared dream and explore realities together.

Imagine yourself in your private dreamworld, walking in the Arctic beside a polar bear. You wake up inside the dream and realize, *I am dreaming!* You turn to the bear, look into his eyes, and you see that he is also awake within the dream. He is sleeping in his world, you are sleeping in yours, and yet you have woken up together in the same dream.

How does it happen that two dreamscapes touch and merge together into one space, in shared awareness? Initially, I mused that the bear and I had wandered to the far reaches of our respective dream territories, found a secret doorway, and opened it to find each other—and a larger way of dreaming. Later, I encountered larger gatherings of lucid dreamers. Several dreams featured a bar called the Meeting Place where visitors came together to converse, share information, and plan adventures. I would come to learn that there are many such shared dream locales where lucid dreamers of different species, from all over the world, meet "undercover" to connect and create.

So, how is this possible? How are such dream locales found? More intriguing, how and why are they created in the first place?

While I find the topic of shared dream space incredibly fascinating, I am not an expert in this field. What follows are my experiences and my ways of understanding what it means to dream with another lucid dreamer or group of dreamers.

When we dream, we enter the world of our imagination (the word derives from the verb *imaginari,* meaning "to picture to oneself"). Shared dream space both draws from and allows for a mutual melding of imaginations. Two or more dreamers meet between realities, in a unique dreamscape environment both created by and discovered through imagination. My perceptions of shared dreamscapes with the bears ranged greatly—from fanciful and humorous to a close approximation of the waking world to mystical settings with cosmic, esoteric overtones.

As dreams of walking beside the polar bear continued, we began to converse and meet in places besides the Arctic. This occurred not only while I was sleeping but also in the light of day. The year of movement in the dreams created an opening in my consciousness, and I found I could slip into a shared dreamscape while resting, walking, or gazing out a window.

I also dreamed of meeting polar bear groups. They went by different names: the Polar Bear Council, Polar Bear Delegation, Polar Bear Contingent. But these are human labels, attempts by the bears to help me classify their intention, voice, or focus. Most of the groups existed in nonphysical frameworks of reality. I thought of some as spirit guides. Some were personal teachers to individual living polar bears; others were mentors or advisors to groups of bears. Some were involved in helping me to meet the polar bear I would come to know as Bering Strait, and some were involved in helping to create this book. They said they had important reasons to arrange for a human and polar bear dreamer to meet: not only to share their story with humans but to reveal what is possible and inspire us all to dream large.

A FEW EXPLANATIONS BEFORE WE BEGIN

Perhaps you are wondering, How can a human understand what a polar bear is thinking? How do you have a conversation with an animal, a group of animals, or animals in spirit form?

I've written several books exploring such topics.[1] When I first learned there were people who conversed with animals, I was curious and skeptical, incredulous at times, yet so very intrigued. How can we connect with a species other than our own to share feelings and opinions and ideas? I interviewed more than two dozen animal communicators and considered frameworks from a variety of paradigms (from quantum physics to shamanism) in an attempt to understand. And then one day, seemingly out of the blue, a small group of birds flew to the bush outside my office window. Without thinking, I raised my hand to my heart, walked toward them, and heard, clear as day, their thoughts inside my head. *Whoa.*

My worldview was changed in an instant, though it would take several years to fully convince myself that my ongoing experiences talking with animals were indeed real. It helped my critical mind to learn that this is not something new. Our ancestors (as well as several cultures still thriving today) both related deeply and communicated fluently with the natural world.

As we open ourselves to the energy that flows through all life, we open ourselves to a deeper form of relationship. We know we share a common awareness with all living beings, for we feel it moving through us, joining us, allowing us to share knowledge and wisdom. By embracing this connection, we open to a simple, natural way of communicating with the world—with mountains and stars, water and stones, with dogs and horses and gorillas and whales. By tapping in to shared awareness, we engage the universal language of life.

For humans obsessed with communicating via cell phones, e-mails, tweets, and twitters, this is not always easy (though it is highly ironic). If we take a break from technological diversions and relax into a quieter, more tranquil state of being, our hurried thoughts and gotta-do-it-this-moment mentality slow down.

Sink deeper still and habitual ways of seeing the world loosen their grip. As rigid judgments about how reality "should be" release their hold, we slide into a more intuitive state, one quite capable of and familiar with the shared language that joins all beings in common understanding.

Call it telepathy. The word derives from *tele,* meaning "distant or far away," and *pathy,* meaning "feeling or perception." Telepathy is feeling from a distance, perceiving from far away. With telepathy we can expand our awareness to connect on inner levels with any other being. Through telepathy we rediscover our fluency in the universal language of mind-to-mind connection and heart-to-heart communication.

We can send and receive telepathic information in a variety of ways. These may include visual images, physical feelings, emotional feelings, inner hearing, intuitive flashes, and deep-down knowing. We may have a preference for one mode over another. If you are very visual, you might deal mostly in pictures and images. If you like to talk and share ideas, you might easily sense an inner translation of words and sentences, which resembles a dialogue. Or, we may blend modes, using the ones that speak most clearly to us in the moment.

Communication with animals is often rich and multilayered. It can also be challenging, for as humans we are limited to our unique sensing mechanisms and brain software. How do we share the goldfish's experience of breathing through gills or the raven's delight of soaring high on open wings? Translating what we sense, feel, and perceive into words and explanations for others to understand is an art that demands clarity as well as creativity.

I've spent well over a decade talking with many individual animals, animal groups, and animals in spirit form. I wrote a book about shapeshifting with animals—that is, shifting the "shape" of one's consciousness so as to perceive the world through an animal's eyes—or feelers or trunk, paws or tentacles.

Before talking with an animal, I feel for the channel, the pathway, the unique frequency that will connect me in deeper relationship—not only with that animal but also with myself. Sometimes I am able to share consciousness, as if I am inside the animal's body, seeing the world from its perspective. I often feel I am in the "passenger seat" in such cases; I am not controlling the animal or attempting to do so, but simply a guest in its bodily vehicle, along for the ride. Other times it is more an interior conversation, as if we are together in a safe, shared space and the animal is telling me about its life.

When I began conversing with the polar bears through dreams, I naturally fell into this familiar mode of connection. But the dreamworld adds another layer to the translation process. While I often remembered the gist of dream conversations (and became quick at jotting down notes upon awakening), the polar bears agreed to help me with recall. Thus, some mornings I would sit down in front of the computer and clear a mental channel for the bears to share their information. Their words flowed through me as I typed, and much of the conversation in following chapters was recorded this way. Working with the bears in this manner was yet another way to connect worlds—not only linking the dreamworld with waking life but opening additional channels of communication between species.

A SHORT PRIOR HISTORY

Although dreaming with groups of polar bears was new for me, talking with a collective polar bear group was not. Just as some dreams set the stage for future meetings, some talks give us an early introduction to things we later need to know.

The first time I spoke with a group of polar bears was in the fall of 2002. There was an unusually large gathering of the bears on the far north coast of Alaska. Wildlife experts weren't sure why it was happening, but it coincided with several international meetings that humans were attending, mostly about environmental issues and how weather changes were affecting our global family.

A friend who edits a Native newsletter asked if I would contact the polar bears for their perspective. Were they gathered because of an abundance of food in that area, or was there another reason, a deeper meaning to this gathering?

I still remember the deep silence that occurred when I initially made contact. I explained to the group that my friend wanted to share their perspective with other humans through her newsletter. I sensed the bears scrutinizing me in a serious manner, as if they were considering not just my request but the thoughts and feelings beneath my words. As I wrote in another book about this, "I felt the largeness of the Polar Bear Spirit, and for a moment I felt so small."[2]

I understood then the depth of their connection—the thoughtful manner in which they spoke, the respect they offered and required in return. It was a good lesson and good training. As you might expect from the animals' great size and bearing, polar bear teaching is Big Medicine.

The polar bear group explained that their meeting was a gathering of energies, similar to human gatherings of peoples from different countries to address the environment and our place in the world. With some humor, the bears noted that their meeting was a reflection of this—or perhaps our meeting was a reflection of theirs.

As the bears put it, *We come together to 'hold' our connections in a new way, both to recharge our bond with each other and with the planet and with the spirit of this particular place. . . . We come here as it is important to us; it is a power place for polar bears you might say. Some humans might explain our gathering in terms of food or the result of storms, but you need to understand that those are human explanations. If you really care to know our point of view, then you must see with the eyes of a polar bear!*[3]

The bears often suggested this idea to me during our talks, and it's a point well made. If we humans truly want to understand the world from another animal's point of view, we need to release our preconceptions, judgments, and human-oriented beliefs. We must shift the shape of our consciousness if we want to see with polar bear eyes.

The bears felt their meeting, as well as the human meetings, were good signs. *"A call to consciousness,"* they put it, a call to greater awareness. They said they were reawakening the deeper medicine they hold and carry for the planet and would be reviewing their role in planetary evolution. Other animals would be doing this as well, they noted. *Many animals are planning, preparing themselves, realigning their interior energies, for changes in the Earth. We do not sense the disasters that are so currently a focus of fear with humans. Rather, our focus is one of conscious awakening. We walk hand in hand, paw in paw, with other creatures of the land—and, yes, with you, the human people, as well.*

We are all pieces of a huge mosaic of planet Earth. As one individual or group of beings opens, another is touched, and then another, and another, and so on, until the pattern becomes a living awareness—an awakening of which we are all part and parcel—one in which we are truly a United Planet of Beings.[4]

I've come to know the Polar Bear people as strong, powerful, loving beings. They are curious, deeply wise, and often very humorous. They also have a unique story and teaching to share, one that affects us all.

7

The Polar Bear Council

We welcome you into our midst. We have walked through your mind and heart, and know your intentions. We are happy to participate, to share our teachings. We welcome the opportunity to speak with humans not only through physical polar bears but as polar bear spirits and representatives of the energetic changes of the Far North.

There are seven of us: six polar bears and me. I am lucid in this dream, sitting with the bears in a circle, inside a giant snow cave. Pale white light radiates from all directions, as if the icy walls, domed top, and snow-packed floor glow from within. There's a peculiar humming noise. It takes me a moment to realize it's the bears talking among themselves. They make no audible sound, but their thoughts buzz as a static hum inside my head. I sense they are waiting for me to hear clearly, but I can't locate the correct frequency. I watch them blink their eyes and turn their necks to regard one another, their gestures slow and fluid. Their fur is tinged yellow, and they seem ancient, calm, and wise. But I also sense this appearance is for my benefit. What do they *really* look like, I wonder? I turn to the bear on my right and watch with fascination as his fur and body become transparent. There's a cosmos inside—black space, dense and dark, with bright swirls of galaxies and stars. How interesting, I think as I feel myself drifting, leaving my body and floating into that space.

I feel pressure on my leg—it's the bear on my right, pressing my knee, bringing me back inside my body with his firm touch. Lucid once again, I am startled by how easy it is to lose focus and drift away in a dream. I direct my attention back to the circle of bears and with focus comes clarity, my inner ears attuning to their thoughts. Satisfied that I am now present, they tell me that they are a special council of spirit bears.

We are part of the Polar Bear Contingent of the Arctic North and beyond, they explain. *We exist in close relationship to physical, living polar bears and in relation to other animals, including humans. We have a specialized manner of connecting with the land and water, with the energy grid of the planet, and with the evolutionary changes the Earth is processing at this time.*

Their voice is deep and strong. I realize they have much to share and begin to worry that I will not remember the details. They continue speaking but silently convey reassurance that they will help with recall.

We are united in that we are all polar bears—or snow bears, sea bears, ice bears, Nanuk, as we are also called by humans. As a common species, we have a united goal: to hold the Earth together, from our position at the top of the world. That has been our purpose for many thousands of lifetimes. We can remember far into the distant past.

We do not divide ourselves by countries as humans do, but by the way our 'lines'—what you might call our paw lines, the paths we use to walk and dream—connect us with the deep earth.

One of our jobs is to help hold the magnetic pole of energy that moves through the planet. There are other such poles, but ours is magnetic in nature. We hold energy in a unique and specialized way that is very important in the shifting of the poles, which is also to say the shifting of duality upon this planet.

Duality, polar opposites, polar bears, Polaris—these human terms and concepts are interrelated to our way of being. We have off-world connections as well as deep-world connections. We help mediate the balance between life under the ice and outer space energies. Polar bears walk certain lines, follow certain paths, not just for food but as means of connecting inner and outer worlds as well as planetary and off-world energies. We are bridgers, connectors. We also work with future lifetimes—though that is another discussion.

Let us begin by addressing the changes our Earth currently is experiencing. We polar bears are in touch with the 'deep people,' or underground spirits of the earth. By this we mean an intelligence that is not often acknowledged by humans, but a sentient intelligence nonetheless. We work with this group of earth beings from time to time. We feel their changes in energetic resonance, just below the surface of the earth.

Currently these deep world beings are in close contact with us about anchoring the Earth for a 'gentle ride' through her shifts and changes. You might think of polar bears as the physical anchors for these deep earth people. We are the anchors that hold their lines—their signature energies—to the surface so that journeys into conscious connection with the deep earth is possible.

As polar bear spirits we share this dream space with you in a similar manner—not only to give voice to our people but also to help create circumstances in which we may offer insights and experiences to that which you, humans, may not be aware. We offer our assistance in this endeavor.

I thank the polar bears, and they look at me, into me, with their deep dark eyes.

We bow our heads to this project, that we may work together to bring our story for humans to hear, to learn and see in a new way. In turn, we learn from you and other humans. All is a circle in this way. This is one example of Polar Bear Medicine and the benefits of what you call conscious dreaming. We will continue this discussion in future meetings. We welcome you to bring questions.

Shortly after our talk ended, I awoke, grabbed my notebook, and began to write. As I later transcribed my notes, I was pleased and reassured to feel the energy of the polar bear group as I typed. I have experienced this with other animals and animal groups. For me, it feels like a helpful energetic presence behind my right shoulder. I often hear an inner voice from the presence that serves to fill in blanks, add details, and—in the case of the polar bears—surprise me with phrases I would suddenly remember from the dream.

Rereading the talk, I noticed how some of their words were encoded with additional layers of meaning, rather like footnotes offering further explanation and details. For example, the bears noted following paw lines, or specialized paths, as they walk and dream. The reference brought to mind the Australian Aboriginal concept of dream tracks, sometimes referred to as song lines. These are paths that reveal the routes creator beings forged in the mythic Dreamtime as they dreamed the world into being. By walking along dream lines with the proper song (or state of consciousness) one may find power spots, sacred connections with dream spirits, and energy vortexes to enable recall of ancient wisdom along the way. This is a topic that has long fascinated me, and I believe the polar bears made use of this "file" within my memories to add a layer of metaphoric explanation so that I would more easily understand what they meant by paw lines. This is also something they would elaborate upon in future talks.

POLAR BEAR DREAMING

The bears had welcomed me to bring questions to our dream meetings. On one level this was a courteous invitation, but I also sensed it as a very strong recommendation. Just as the bears were able to sniff out the feelings and thoughts behind my words, I felt the serious overtone behind their request.

It's an important reminder in any relationship, of course; we need to pull our end, to bring our full attention and inquisitiveness to such exchanges of information. Conversation is not meant to be a one-way street. I've met many animal species who are curious about the human animal and welcome opportunities to learn more. The Polar Bear Council made it clear that I was to take an active role in our conversation.

We will speak about dreams, the group announced several nights later. Once again, we were in the snow cave, in a circle, the same soft white light glowing from the walls and floor.

You could say that we help to awaken living (physical) bears in the dreamworld to advanced techniques. All polar bears have the ability to dream consciously—this is part of Polar Bear Medicine, though some bears are more accomplished than others. We mostly work with bears who have advanced abilities. We also work with humans. In the past, we worked with many human dreamers, medicine people, or shamans who learned to join our dreamworld. Part of Polar Bear Medicine is to bring awareness of this dreamworld to humans.

We have for a long time wished to connect in deeper ways with more humans; though, the timing is yours to acknowledge. We are available, we are open. It is for humans to ask, to humble their consciousness so as to see all that they do not see. This . . . pride . . . is often a destructive force with humans, this sense of thinking you know better, of believing your way is the only way.

The dreamworld reveals this is not the case; there are many possible realities, many worlds, and many ways to see and feel and be with others. We offer this as a great learning lesson—as do many other species when working with humans. To join with us in the dream is to awaken a bit, to begin to incorporate a larger view of consciousness so that remembering can occur.

Now, bring us your questions.

Where to start? I thought for a moment. "Can you tell me more about the polar bear way of dreaming and how this type of dreaming relates to humans?"

Polar bear dreaming is not something we consider separate from our lives. We have observed human dreaming and note that it is often com-partmentalized from your waking day. For polar bears this is not so. We have what you might term 'fluid dreaming,' for it moves with us as we move throughout our life, day and night.

One difference between humans and polar bears is that movement and dreaming are very much a part of our lives. We mean movement in a deep sense—our paws and bellies centered deep within the earth, below the crust, below the waters, our dreaming awareness in touch with the deep earth peoples.

Our connection with these energies—and with off-world energies—is tied in to our role as dreaming bears. We bridge many realities: land and sea, fluid sea and iced sea, which is often like land. We chose to walk these quiet, windswept areas, to commune with whale and walrus, seals and many of the creatures who live on the land, birds and fox, and other beings whom you do not name.

"What type of other beings?" I asked.

There are energies that humans do not recognize. In older times some human peoples knew these energies and gave them names: wind energies and starlight energies; aurora energies that come to Earth and dance upon the ice; sea energies that swirl around us and speak to us too. So many energies in a land that humans often refer to as barren. Perhaps what you really mean is 'bear-in,' for we are the bear in the barren lands.

I laughed and for a moment felt myself laughing in my sleeping body, in bed, as well. I knew—and would further experience—that the bears were fond of such puns. They had a sharp, clever wit, and I sensed their good-natured amusement with our language, for the humorous yet aptly fitting ways certain words and phrases corresponded to ideas they wished to discuss.

We wish to speak of the connection between human and polar bear dreaming. Let us approach this as you understand the concept of Bear Medicine. Conscious dreaming is part of our medicine, one of our talents. It is also a gift that at this time we offer to humans who are hungry to learn new ways and reawaken to what they know they know, but do not know.

The bears paused and I pondered their meaning.

We are referring to movement within the dreamworld as it touches the waking world of humans, which is not waking at all, as we see it. To be awake is to be aware of all the worlds, just as it is to be aware of the sentience of all peoples—stones and stars, seals and polar bears.

We do not wish to be heavy with blame. That is not our intention. We wish to open pathways of communication between us. To open the lines of dream songs that encircle the Earth and unite us as the fellow beings in awakening that we are.

We leave you with this for now. And we will speak more of the dream that is awakening.

A POLAR BEAR MYTH

I enjoyed talking with the Polar Bear Contingent and had several more snow-cave dreams—some lucid, some not. The bears also continued to share information during the day, while I was at my computer. Sometimes I would sense their desire to talk. Other times I would simply be wondering about a question and they would answer in the moment or at a later date. I did my best to listen because I knew they were listening to me, too.

One day while preparing an exercise for an upcoming animal communication workshop, I recalled a myth shared by a group of musk oxen. The herd I had spoken to considered themselves "bridgers"—animals who serve to bridge the ancient past with the present and future. Musk oxen are a very old species, with a long history of traveling across many lands and forming an intimate relationship with the Earth. *We have a conscious connection to our role as a species that spans time,* they related. *That information is available to us in any moment, and it is easy for us to connect with this . . . We enjoy stories, especially those of our travels and of all the history Earth stores within our bones.*[1] The musk oxen then offered to share one of their myths.

Reading this made me think of the polar bears and how they also thought of themselves as bridgers, connectors between the deep earth people and the skies, and perhaps between past and future as well. I wondered if the polar bears had a mythic story of dreaming, or perhaps of coming into existence, that they would share. The next morning, I felt the Polar Bear Council's familiar presence and an answer.

As for myths, they began, *we are familiar with this form of storytelling. It is similar to a specialized form of dreaming that we will speak about later. But for now, here is a simple 'myth' about how our connections with off-world energies began.*

In the early, early days polar bears dreamed themselves up from their sleeping bodies to sail among the stars. This was not unusual. It was—and is—our joy to move our dream bodies through water, snow, wind, and air. We often swam through the waves of the northern lights, diving in and out, enjoying big bear somersaults in the sky.

In one dream, we flew high, very far, and were surprised to meet energies not of the Earth. These were Polar Bear people, like ourselves, dream swimming through the night sky. They lived upon another planet, a star you call Polaris.

The bear beings of Polaris spoke to us in ways similar to sea creatures. In the beginning, we didn't understand their manner of speaking. Theirs was a toning call, a kind of singing—more whale or seal than polar bear, but since we are familiar with the songs of the whales and seals, we began to understand.

The bear people of Polaris told us they had once dreamed themselves to our planet to hold the world together from the top of the world. This was surprising to us. "We are your dream?" we asked them, and they said, no not exactly, "because a dream once dreamed acquires a life of its own and so becomes a living being—just as you are living beings who have evolved in your own way. We come to greet you, to dance with you and share our stories, and to learn of yours."

And so began the relationship between polar bears and the Polar Bear people. We are now one being, and this is how we acquired some of the off-world knowledge that we have today. Not only as physical polar bears having lived upon the Earth, but also as members of the Polar Bear Contingent, a dream that stretches paw to paw across the sea and sky. This is also who we are.

I thanked the bears and sat still for quite some time. Their myth was like an ancient dream, a fragile story that is best held lightly. Its significance reminded me how I had tried to see what the bears really looked like in the snow cave and discovered a cosmos living inside a bear spirit, inside a lucid dream. Myths, like dreams, can offer transport to strange and wonderful places. And some of these places can only be experienced through special vibrations of consciousness. If we want to understand the secrets of such exotic locales, we would be wise to learn—and appreciate—the subtleties of the language.

We like the idea of sharing stories of who we are and how we experience the world, not just as how humans experience us, the bears added gently. *We have many insights that we will share. We invite you to journey with us, to see through our eyes. We lend you our thoughts and vision. We share our energies to help your words sing with the song of Polar Bear.*

8

Entering the Dream

While I very much enjoyed talking with the Polar Bear Council and found their information fascinating, I continued to wonder about the lone white bear who had walked beside me for so long in my dreams. Even though my lucid encounter with that bear had only lasted a few seconds, I was keen to see him again, to reestablish our personal connection through the shared dreamscape.

In truth, I sometimes felt a bit intimidated by the solemn, slightly impersonal demeanor of the council. I had not yet decided to write this book, and yet the group continued to refer to our "project" and seemed intent on sharing information meant for a large audience.

They also asked questions I didn't have precise answers to, particularly questions regarding my consciousness during dreaming: How did I enter and exit a dream? Could I dream myself directly into a waking dream? Could I walk from one dreamscape into another? Could I find their ice cave, for example, from another part of the dream? Although I sometimes found these questions bewildering, I knew the bears were nudging me to be more observant of the nuances of dreams, to be more consciously aware and involved with the process of dreaming.

The Polar Bear Council continued to encourage me to ask questions as well. However, I sensed they were occasionally annoyed with my interviewing skills, especially when they replied brusquely, as if the answer to the question should be self-evident: Why is this ice cave glowing? *Because it is alive!*

I respected those ancient dream bear spirits, and knew it was an honor to sit with them, that they trusted me to prepare their words for widespread sharing. But I also felt unsure of myself, uncertain of my ability to translate their message, and aware of the many obstacles involved in such a project. At times, I felt lost.

One afternoon while reading *Ensouling Language,* a book about the art of nonfiction writing, a sentence leaped out and spoke directly to my soul. The author of the book, Stephen Harrod Buhner, had been discussing the unique rhythm of movement in which deeper meaning emerges and develops through the writing process. When good writing works, readers are led not only to the writer's intimate view of reality but into a true, deep encounter with themselves. The spirit of the book resonates, opening the heart and mind, awakening something within. As Buhner notes, however, in order for writing to work in the first place, the writer must undergo a similar process. He or she must feel deeply, engaging subtle sensory mechanisms, listening for what the book wants to say. And yet, just as a writer discovers what is true by writing it, just as a dreamer discovers what is real by dreaming it, here's the catch: we don't know in advance what this is, this *truth* that is trying to speak to us or through us. As I read Buhner's personal sharing and wise observation, I felt heartened and inspired and reassured. "We all enter the dream not really knowing where we're going."[1]

That night there was another dream. I sit in the same circle, with the bears, in the snow cave with the beautiful, pale glow. But light does not emanate from all directions, for in the middle of the floor is a polar bear skin, opaquely obscuring the light below. The skin is flat in the middle, slightly rounded in the paws and claws, only the faintest hint of past life in the pert ears, tunneled snout, and slightly open mouth.

The council seems not to mind this dead bear in the center of their midst. Quiet and composed, they look at me, their expressions curious and slightly amused. *Bring us your questions,* they say.

"Is that someone you know?" I surprise myself with voicing such a sassy attitude. But once the question tumbles out, a floodgate opens, letting loose my doubts and reservations. "Are there really living polar bears who work with human dreamers? Am I projecting this idea, or misinterpreting it, or is this the way you understand it too? Are you guiding the way I interpret these dreams? Like this snow cave, for example—is the way I see it in this dream the way you sense it too? How can I know? What can I do to understand better?" My questions taper off as the big white bear sitting across from me holds up his paw, reminding me of the dream professor who once quieted me with a look.

We will answer as a group to begin. The idea of special 'dreaming bears' is not wholly your own, though the way you have conceived of it belongs to your view of the world. Many of the ideas you have been thinking of in connection with polar bears are not projections, but shared ideas from the Polar Bear people. This is the beginning of a greater sharing that we would like to explore.

For us, there have always been bears who walk in several worlds, both on the physical Earth and in the stars. There are also bears who work with humans (and other species) in special ways. And yes, there are dreams and dreamers who are aided and supported by the dream contingent.

The dreams you've experienced of walking beside a bear in the Arctic are not wholly your own, but a match created out of need and available connection. Your ability to translate and write about animal thoughts in human terms was paired with the need for more humans to 'hear' from more animal species on our planet. In addition, your desire to learn as a dreamer was paired with the ability of a particular dreaming bear.

We offer you the gift of dreaming. This is a key to our work together— the value of dreaming to walk together, to share our wisdom, and for you to share yours. This is how we envision this project, this book: a sharing of wisdom together.

Our insight is that you must allow yourself to become vulnerable and open. Risk asking questions and risk giving answers. Risk finding the deeper you. We offer you the movement of dreaming together, with us.

We will begin by tuning—or attuning—your consciousness closer to ours. This is the reason you walked with the bear in your dreams for some time, to match the movement of the polar bear as you begin to deepen in your life and the interior life of the dream.

There is one among us who has familiarity with the world of the human, the world of the polar bear, the world of the High Dream Bear Council, and a walker between worlds. He offers his aid in helping you to understand the life of such a unique bear. He will begin.

BERING STRAIT

I watch with fascination as the flat bear skin in the middle of the circle plumps up in the middle, as if something big and round is pushing upward from beneath the floor. The bears in the circle snort noisy puffs of air and rock their big bodies back and forth, like old men laughing. Is this some technique, I wonder? Are they making this happen? But my gaze returns to the middle of the circle, to the living polar bear taking shape, slowly at first: front leg and paw stretching outward, neck gliding round, snout turning toward me, and those bright, dark eyes—the ones I have seen before, in a dream.

My name is Bering Strait. He speaks calmly, both to the group of bears and with a nod toward me. *This is a name I chose for you. Humans enjoy names and this name has many meanings. I also have many meanings, as I travel simultaneously in several worlds.*

I pinch my fingers to stay present in the dream, to not get too excited that here at last is the bear. Did he dream himself into the cave? I focus on his words, to take in what he is telling me. I have the sense that he has prepared what he is to say.

As a living polar bear, I walk near the coast of the Chukchi Sea. I was born in this area and have traveled long distances to many places, including Alaska. These are human names for the regions I traverse.

I am also aware of and connected to the Polar Bear Contingent—a larger aspect of this group—and serve as a link to the physical world of polar bears. I will share more on that later if you desire. This council has granted me permission to discuss more about my work with them and what they—we—do.

I am a dreaming bear. This means I have certain skills in extending myself through the dreamworlds. Many polar bears carry this medicine, though some to a greater extent than others. I am a special dreamer in that I am dreaming not only of polar bear evolution but the coevolution of our planet. And for that I have been instructed to make contact with human dreamers, to 'put out the word' so to speak in order to set alight the consciousness of this planet.

This is not a new concept and many different animal species currently participate in this adventure. Some humans converse with animals and convey their feelings and insights; some share our stories; and some forge deeper relationships with animals, not simply from a biological, scientific viewpoint but as partners, friends. And there are humans who dream with animals, too.

I have been asked to share my life with you and I make myself available for us to converse. I can dictate some experiences from my present life and we can share others in dreams. Together we will forge a story that speaks not only to the mind but to the hearts of humans. We—this Polar Bear Council—invite the human people to engage in deeper, more authentic relationships with the Earth and all creatures.

We also would like to share insights from the polar bear perspective, certain insights that you may know something about but not all. We find humans sometimes see part of the truth, but because of their blockages in consciousness, do not see the whole vision.

So, we offer you a walk with polar bears so as to see our world more clearly, more completely. And so we wander into your dreams, into your stream of consciousness, and across your mind's eye, through your thoughts, into your words to reach the eyes and ears of others. For this we are pleased and honored. We hope to please and honor you, that you will be honored by us. In light and friendship, you may call me Bering Strait.

BEARING STRAIGHT

Bering Strait—the name made me smile. I was touched that the bear had chosen a special name for me to call him, even if it was simply because "humans enjoy names." Soon after transcribing our talk, I began to ponder this moniker of many meanings and, because I am human, enjoy.

To begin with the obvious, Bering Strait is the name of a narrow, shallow channel of water between Siberia and Alaska, just south of the polar circle. The strait links two continents as well as two oceans: the easternmost point of Asia with the westernmost point of North America, the Pacific and the Arctic (via the Chukchi Sea). It gets its name from Vitus Bering, a Danish-born Russian explorer who captained several naval expeditions seeking to find clear seas between Russia and America. Once long ago, during an ice age when sea levels fell, the strait served as a land bridge, allowing for the migration of animals between Asia and North America. More recently, the frozen strait has been walked across, skied across, and even driven across by humans. The strait separates and connects, delineates and bridges. Fittingly, the international date line runs through the middle of the strait.

But Bering Strait is also a homonym for *bearing straight*—moving forward, in one direction, without curve or swerve or bend. *Bearing* may signify relevance or support. As a navigation term, *bearing* means being aware of one's position in relation to one's surroundings. To bear is to carry, to display, to produce knowledge, fruit, or offspring. We can bear arms, bear witness, bear scrutiny, bear a grudge, or simply grin and bear it. And what of *straight*? Straight is proper, level, upright, symmetrical, the shortest distance between two points. Straight is honest, frank, and forthright. Straight thinking is clear; a straight gaze is steady, nononsense, and bold. Straight can mean directly, right now, straight away.

Bering Strait, bearing straight. I spoke the words aloud, and another homonym came to mind: baring straight. Perhaps we only progress in dreams, and life, by baring ourselves in ever greater degrees—by uncovering judgments and assumptions, by letting go of old ideas and outdated beliefs. Just as the council once reminded me of the bear in the barren Arctic, so too was there a sense of essential truths, straightforward talk, and bare facts in the way the bears related to me. I understood their desire for reciprocation.

As I jotted notes, I let my thoughts simmer, considering how all these meanings might apply to the polar bear who walked beside me in my dreams. Play with words and they will show you all sorts of things, uncovering secrets, revealing unexpected meanings, engaging you with delight—such as that bold bit of humor hiding plainly in the initials chosen for this name, *BS*.

During the next few weeks I happily dream walked beside the polar bear who called himself Bering Strait. Conversation flowed easily between us, though many times we were quiet, taking pleasure in a still communion that left me waking refreshed and encouraged.

Sometimes I was lucid in the dreams, sometimes not, and other times I was surprised to awaken partway through the dream. I remembered the council's recommendation to take notice, to be aware of the transitional zones between dreaming and awakening.

In one dream, we were walking as we had before, side by side, across a snowy plain. There was a twilight cast of colors—subdued blues and purples—and a blur of low mountains along the horizon.

As Bering Strait was talking, I had the impression he was repeating himself. I knew my dreaming mind strayed at times, and I would lose focus, distracted by the shape of a snow formation, the way a particular shade of light imbued the scene, or, lately, the mysterious high-pitched hum that Bering identified as the song of sea ice.

Let us be clear about who I am, he was saying. *In the consensus reality you know as the waking world, I am physically embodied as a mature male bear. And yet, much of 'me' is also available as a conscious connection between different worlds.*

My job is to help you to understand the world of the polar bear through our eyes; to understand the deeper vision we hold of both our kind and our roles on Earth; and to forge a deeper relationship between humans and polar bears so as to create a more conscious connection between all peoples living upon this Earth.

"How do we begin?" I asked. I had learned to ask questions not only for information but also as a way to stay present in the dream. When there was no reply, I glanced his way and noticed the slight rise of his snout, pointing to the left. Following the direction, I saw a domed, glowing object hovering just above the ice in the far distance. There was a spaceship quality to the object, but there was something familiar too, and then I realized—it was the glowing ice cave. This is what the council meant by finding their cave from "another part of the dream."

"This is how we start!" I heard an echo of my words spoken aloud— with exclamation in the dream and as murmur through my sleeping body. The sound was a vehicle of consciousness, a kind of interworld connection, and layers of understanding began to fall in place. A secret was unfolding, something I knew but couldn't fully articulate. I felt a deep well of gratitude to the dreaming bear beside me and to the council, too. I felt the presence and love of many beings, smiling, glowing, alive.

Become a polar bear person, suggested Bering once again. *Walk with us and dream with us and begin to live with us, within us, to see our world. That is the gist of our experiential gift to you: to see from our eyes.*

You do not know the full picture because you have not yet fully seen from our eyes. We have many mysteries and stories to share. Why not become a polar bear person yourself so as to share what it is that we are and how we live in the world?

Walk like a polar bear, move like a polar bear, think like a polar bear and you will know the polar bear story to share. We support your movements inward to join us in this adventure!

9

What We Know and What We Don't Know

Despite the bears' ongoing encouragement and enticing proposal to become a "polar bear person," I continued to feel hesitant and skeptical at times. Their purpose was to share a polar bear perspective—and yet, I was being so typically human.

A HUMAN PERSPECTIVE

In an attempt to ground myself with knowledge, arm myself with facts and figures, and make better sense of what I was learning, I began to read all I could find about polar bears. This had mixed results.

On the one hand, polar bear research offers many diverse facts. We know where polar bears roam and what they eat, how they den and when they sleep. We know their average weight and height and life expectancy, the length and thickness of tooth and claw, the percentage of milk fat mother bears produce, and much, much more. Certainly, human information about polar bears is helpful to categorize, quantify, and comprehend.

On the other hand, the more thoroughly we analyze the animal, the more we distance ourselves from relationship. Wrapped up in details, facts, and statistics, we forget to open our hearts and pay attention to feelings. It's a strange inversion: the more we think we know about polar bears, the less we see them as they truly are.

Of the many books I read about polar bears, my favorites were written by Nikita Ovsyanikov, a Russian researcher who lived among the white bears for many years. Ovsyanikov has a way with bears. Armed with only a stick and a well-honed understanding of polar bear behavior and mannerisms, he walked freely among them. "I believe if we treat polar bears with care and respect, they are far less likely to hurt us than we are to hurt them with our thoughtless and careless ways," he wrote.[1]

Ovsyanikov is a keen observer and one of the few researchers who questioned some of the long-standing beliefs humans hold about polar bears. Several of his observations stand in direct contradiction to conventional portrayals of the bears that have been passed on for generations. For example, a commonly held notion is that male polar bears are especially aggressive toward female bears and will attack, kill, and eat their cubs. Ovsyanikov, who has recorded more than five hundred exchanges with the bears during his many years of living with them in the high Arctic, never witnessed this type of behavior. Rather, his many observations reveal that female bears are the more aggressive, charging and striking at nearby males, who "always retreated."[2]

Much of what you have been reading is accurate, the Polar Bear Council commented one evening, referring to one of the books by Ovsyanikov. *We helped to draw that book to you because we know of this man and his manner of seeing polar bears, not only through his eyes but by extending his consciousness and seeing through our eyes as well.*

This remark caused me to reflect and realize something very important. While my reading helped me learn more about polar bears, it did not help with the main task the polar bears proposed: to see through their eyes.

We have been watching your energies and attempting to inspire you with our thoughts, they said. *As you know, polar bears are movers. We walk and are almost continually on the move. We see your hesitations, your many moments of hibernation.*

Indeed, for many months my conversation with the bears had been mostly on hold, the shared dreaming hesitant from my end. I had lost direction and sometimes retreated within. Hibernation was a good way to describe it (though as any good book about *Ursus maritimus* will inform you, polar bears are not true hibernators).

We see you walking in circles—a kind of polar bear walk, sniffing the air to determine what to do. You are cautious, yet curious. This, too, is a polar bear trait.

We do not write books. We are polar bear people. But we extend our paws to you as a 'pause' in your thinking process, your circling process.

Polar bears know how to wait. We are patient people, as are you. Some of your thoughts are not patient, however, and we see you worrying about others.

It was true; I had fallen into the bad habit of judging and comparing my experiences to those of others. I was looking for common ground, but my encounters with the bears were anything but common. Our project ventured into uncharted territory—a coming together of worlds and species through shared dreaming. I needed to let go of comparisons, judgments, and vague ideas of what should be. And yet, it was sometimes difficult to ignore the background static, all that self-doubt buzzing through my mind.

There is no joy in this, the bears agreed. *We each have our own way. This is something polar bears have learned and part of the reason we walk alone, not in a group. Still, there is joy in coming together with other bears to share a feast of whale or walrus.*

Part of our purpose is connecting with humans—not as skins on walls or mounts in museums or photographs in books but as living, thinking, sentient, spiritual, dreaming bears who offer our help to you at this time.

We are a strong dreaming. Our dreaming is not for everyone, and yet because of our power and the nature of the power we hold at the top of the world, we affect all beings. This is something humans only vaguely understand.

If polar bears leave, who will hold the energy of the Earth from the North? We have much to do with the health of the Earth and our planetary connection with the stars. We have powerful polar bear dreaming, but, as such, it requires a certain power and spiritual maturity to unlock this door, this door to polar bear wisdom.

You must first be opened, your door unlocked, so that a dreaming bear might slip in and take up residence. Perhaps he nudges you into the heart of a dream and shows you the life of a living polar bear. Then you begin to learn not just of the science or observation of polar bears but how to think, feel, and sense as a polar bear. This is the larger myth awakening.

We have several myths to share with you—'big dreams' you might call them—stories and understandings that speak of the interwinding of polar bear and human myths. Can you open yourself wide enough to hear and see such a vision? We hope so!

Through the magic of merging myths and dreams, something happens not only to you and human people but to our Bering Strait—and us, as well.

This is the new adventure. This is the way it begins. Think of your early Arctic explorers—a few curious souls who adventure to vistas not seen before. Some people will claim their trek is foolish or impossible, but the adventurer hears the call. Just as the dreamer hears the call of the dream and responds. This is our awakening.

Trust yourself. That is the greatest advice we can offer you now. We are here with you and support your endeavors. We protect you and share our wisdom too.

A DIFFERENT PERSPECTIVE

As usual, the Polar Bear Council left me with plenty to consider, and plenty of questions. Do we hear the call of the dream? Are we capable of opening ourselves to the larger myth awakening? What happens to us, and the Earth, if polar bears leave the planet?

Human opinion varies widely regarding polar bears as an endangered species on the edge of extinction. The polar bear has become the troubled face of global warming—and warning. Loss of sea ice means less access to seals and larger distances between ice floes; this means less food for the bears, a great chance of exhaustion while swimming, and possible drowning. Stress, declining birth rates, overhunting, pollution—the polar bears' potential demise is debated with a slew of statistics and hot, heartfelt emotions. But what do we really know?

In 2014, there were an estimated twenty thousand to twenty-five thousand polar bears worldwide. Their range covers Arctic areas of five countries: Canada, United States, Russia, Greenland/Denmark, and Norway. Scientists recognize nineteen distinct subpopulations of polar bears. Part of the confusion of contrary reports about polar bear endangerment is that these populations fluctuate: some are in decline, some are growing, and others remain the same.

And yet—however many details we consider, this is simply one perspective, and very obviously human. As the Polar Bear Council related, they distinguish themselves not by countries or geographic areas but by the way their paw lines connect them to the earth. What else do they see differently? Do polar bears consider themselves to be on the brink of extinction?

We will address this idea of being endangered, the council began one morning. *Polar bears do not regard this in the same way that humans do. Many, many animals see the human animal as the most endangered. We concur. From our perspective, humans are at the top of the endangered species list. We mean this in the sense of conscious thoughts going awry, a species lost in sleepwalking illusion. This is not dreaming as we know it but a sickness that leads to loss of balance and spirit.*

There was a long pause, and I sensed the bears contemplating, considering the direction of our conversation. I also sensed the council sensing me—reading my thoughts, gauging my energy, determining my ability to take in the significance of their message. Something big was coming.

Several days later, the bears invited me to journey with them. It began as a simple attempt to see like a polar bear, to view the Arctic from the perspective of a living bear. What started as "a small adventure," however, soon became something remarkable. I have encountered similar shifts with other animals, and often with the bears. A casual talk suddenly deepens in focus, an individual voice flows into a larger group voice—a voice of species or ancestor or ancient spirit—along with an expanded view. The dream bears had a subtle ability to engage me with story or adventure—and then, skillfully, gracefully, deepen the resonance, fine-tune conscious connections, helping me to see more completely, more precisely in alignment with their unique perspective.

If you are open to a new experience, perhaps you will consider accepting the following invitation to walk beside a polar bear, to shift your awareness, to consider a different perspective, and perhaps, to understand who we are from another point of view. For, as the bears have so often told me, this is also for you.

We invite you today for a small adventure walking as a polar bear. We begin our movement on a flat expanse of the frozen Arctic Ocean, far from land. The days are turning darker. You see through the eyes of a large male bear on his own. You are strong and have much stamina. You have learned the art of hunting seals. This is not only a necessity but also a challenge that is sometimes filled with pleasure. You connect yourself with the Seal people and feel into their energy. You know where the seals frequent their breathing holes in this area. You tune in to these places—you hear them, feel them, smell them—and you stop and wait.

Still, seals are always surprising. They have habits, just as polar bears do—just as humans do—but the Seal people are a clever match for polar bears and that is why we respect and honor them. By eating seals, we become Seal and learn of the Seal people's knowledge. By being eaten, the seals become part of us. We learn from each other in this way.

Polar bears can be very patient when attending to seals. We wait and watch and feel. We can smell their presence, we watch for their breathing; we sense them through our paws, and sometimes through the hairs on our faces and legs.

The connection between seals and polar bears is ancient, and polar bears have myths of the Seal people, just as the seals hold stories of the Polar Bear people. There is mutual respect between us. It is a cycle of ever becoming that we follow, that we participate within, seals and polar bears.

In this same way, we also know of whales and walrus, and some land animals, birds, and sea plants as well. Mostly we know of seals, whales, and walrus. We do not generally hunt whales (sometimes belugas, the white whales) but when whale carcasses are available to us, we eat and learn of whale in this way. So, too, we hear the songs of the whales and learn of their movements beneath the sea.

Whales and polar bears share a common history through being hunted by whalers and humans who harmed us—and themselves—more than they could know. Those humans did not respect the ways of the hunter; they took more than they needed and mistreated our people and the Whale people in ways that were foreign to us. The whales endured many, many generations of shock, and polar bears were also soul saddened by this action of our old friends, the humans.

This is when we knew the human people had forgotten too much, that their explorations had turned sick and sad, that they had wandered too far from their souls, their minds and hearts darkened and diseased.

We learned this was happening all over the Earth, to many different animals. The humans had lost their way, wearing fur or feathers not for warmth, not in the spirit of shared knowledge or mutual give and take, not with respect but for arrogant show and greed. It was as if the humans desired to cover up the dreadful loss from their souls, as if to say to the world, we are strong and powerful and beautiful—but in such a false, sad way that could never cover their shame at having wandered so far from themselves.

For a very long time this dark arena filled the heart of mankind— a strange human word, we think, for man is often not very kind at all.

Many of the ancient ones also lost their way; they did not hunt us with respect. They no longer called to us as they once did; they no longer honored us with gifts or dance. They skinned us nearly alive and sent our skins far away from our home on the ice, allowing our meat to waste.

Animals do not hold the same emotions as humans, and different animals hold different points of view, different relationships and feelings toward the world and humans. For polar bears, we wanted only to be alone, on our own, to do our work.

We were saddened to lose our connection with the human people—whom we once taught to hunt seal and stalk and move unseen upon the ice and snow. We once shared many secrets with shaman people, though now few called to us. We were no longer in alliance with human hunters or even groups of humans to protect.

Polar bears took a soul retreat, going about our living away from humans, escaping your species as best we could. We were no longer in alliance to help.

There was one group, however—a small group of dreaming bears that held fast to the notion that humans would one day return to the circle of life. Polar bear wisdom is very strong, they asserted, and the alliance with humans would be needed one day.

These bears formed a contingent—a contingency if things went too bad, too far astray. These were dream bears who sometimes lived as physical bears who lived and died, but also as spirit bears, and always their spirit was connected to the dream contingent. Its job was to fashion and hold a way for humans to stay connected to polar bears, a way for us to share our wisdom once again, when it was time.

Only in the recent past have humans again come to wonder about polar bears. Some of your trophy hunts have stopped. Some of the Native northern hunters now remember to call to us. It is as if the past is coming back, a little at a time, though not, as expected, in the same ways.

Now there are scientists who come. We understand their hearts do not mean harm, that they are trying to learn of polar bears, but we will tell you this—you cannot really know of polar bears through shooting us with paralysis, by stealing our blood or milk or teeth or fat or fur. You do not even ask our permission! This, too, is a shameful act, one devoid of respect and honor, and so all you get is the superficial life of a polar bear, none of our secrets, none of our wisdom.

There are a very few who come to live among us, to walk as a polar bear, to learn to live and see and smell and feel like a polar bear. It is to these humans that we dedicate our efforts to share our lives, and some of our secrets.

And now there is a group of dreamers who come to us, to share in the dream contingent's plan to learn of polar bears and their ways, and by this, to create a new opening in the world. Not only between polar bears and humans but between all beings united in the web of life and with the Earth.

The time is now. And thus we offer the dream to you. This is our dear dream to you.

With Love,
The Polar Bear Contingent

10
How to Catch a Seal

As encouragement and reminder to continue honing my skills, the Polar Bear Council offered a new challenge: Wake up inside a dream and find "the Meeting Place." Although they didn't explain what or where the Meeting Place was, I understood it to be a mutually accessible dream locale, where two or more dreamers could meet within the same dreamworld.

When I asked for pointers, the bears suggested that the search was an essential part of the learning. More and more I sensed the council's firm yet supportive paw in nudging me toward keener observation and self-confidence. Although I was able to join in lucid awareness with both Bering and the council, I didn't have much control—I simply awoke to connection within the dream. Were the bears helping me to achieve this? Perhaps they were responsible all along, guiding me into those initial dreams of walking beside the polar bear in the Arctic. I remembered how Bering Strait assisted with the council's first challenge, pointing out their distant ice cave from our location in the dream. It was time to try on my own.

With "Meeting Place" in mind before I went to sleep, I dreamed of walking along a road not far from my house. In waking life, the road paralleled a trail often used by Iditarod dog mushers, and in the dreams

I would sometimes hear the muffled sounds of dog teams running in the distance. Although it was early fall, the dream settings were always winter's night—dark sky, bright moon, silvery snow. The energy of the dreams was calm and contemplative. Several times I became lucid and remembered the directive—*find the Meeting Place!*—but all I noticed was the road, the sky, the trees, and snow and, sometimes, small animal holes along the trail.

After several repetitions of the same basic dream, I reread the entries in my journal. I was looking for clues, something unusual—perhaps the holes? Although they were such a small detail, I sensed I might be on to something.

I recalled a recurring dream from my early twenties. I was in a large gymnasium, training with an instructor. The man was short, old, slight of build, but his body conveyed a powerful sense of presence and authority. We stood together at one end of the gym; on the other end was an aquarium, about eight feet long by two feet high. It was elevated on a stand, as home aquariums often are, the top of the tank shoulder height. The test was to run very fast across the room and, at the last moment, turn sideways, lean backward, and kick up both legs so as to be perfectly horizontal with the tank and then slide into the aquarium. I was frightened to do this and didn't really believe it possible, but the instructor was adamant. The secret, he said, was to sense the opening in the center of the aquarium. By running fast and trusting my movements, the energy in my body would attune to its resonance and I would slide in easily. Despite my fear and disbelief, I ran fast, trusted the movement, and slid into the aquarium just as the instructor promised.

That evening I had an equally demanding, yet comparable dream. I am standing next to an old pub on the corner of two cobbled streets in a European city. The air is chilled and misty, and there is a large dark puddle on the road in front of me. A wonderful party is taking place inside the pub, but I cannot get there by walking through the door. The only way to join the party is by diving head first into the big dark puddle.

On waking, I remembered having stared at this puddle several times before. Consulting my journals, I found five dreams from my early thirties in which I stood on the same street, looking down at the puddle. In each dream, I knew a secret: by lifting my arms overhead, jumping high in the air, flipping my feet upward, and diving headlong into the puddle, I would enter the warm, golden light of the pub to enjoy the party. There was always a moment of hesitation, however. Just as in the aquarium dream, I was fearful, not fully believing the task was possible, yet also knowing that any attempt other than full commitment—a fast-running horizontal slide, a head-first dive—would fail.

When I next spoke with Bering Strait, I shared the dreams of walking along the road, noticing the animal holes, and recalling the aquarium and pub dreams.

You are observing the icebergs of your greater being, Bering observed. *What you are looking for is a hole—a way in.*

"Exactly," I said, although I wondered, what are the icebergs of my greater being? Fear of moving forward, of diving into the puddle, sliding into the aquarium, actually finding the Meeting Place?

You want to discover where to locate the hole, how to find the Meeting Place. You are hunting!

I considered the idea. It wasn't how I saw myself, but Bering Strait seemed excited with the comparison.

Do you know what polar bears do when we hunt? We look for a hole that is made by a seal—a breathing hole. That is the way we find food—nourishment and energy. Have you found a seal hole?

A seal's breathing hole—I supposed it was as good a metaphor as any of my dream images (an aquarium, a street puddle) for finding the entrance to the Meeting Place. And I was searching—hunting—for a special place within the dream, a unique resonance that was invisible, subtle as seal breath. But if these were my clues, what was I to do with them?

You must have the patience of a polar bear to watch the hole, sensing for signs of breath. And then—you pounce! You only have one chance, so it is important to remember: patience and timing.

I recalled the dream of dancing with the polar bear and how by "freezing" I was forced to stay present, not run away, and wait for the unfolding—the sweet spot of the dream, the final moment of recognition that launched me into the polar bear's arms. *Patience and timing.* Lessons learned? Trust the dream; trust yourself.

I will watch with you, said Bering. *Breathe deep and watch and listen and feel throughout all your being. That is how you catch a seal.*

THE BOOK OF SMELLS

I continued to work on dreaming myself to the Meeting Place, that fabled nexus of dream sharers. I was fascinated by the challenge and kept my eyes peeled for breathing holes, yet my dreams kept taking me to the road not far from my home. These were peaceful dreams of silvery moonlight and glimmering snow. It felt good to walk, to know I was dreaming, tranquil yet attentive to where the Meeting Place might be found. I no longer saw holes along the trail, but I discovered a marvelous ability to leap high and far. The discovery came by accident one night as I tripped. I could feel myself in bed—feet stumbling, legs jerking forward. In an attempt to stay lucid within the dream, I imagined myself sailing upward. And so it happened: a lofty, graceful, fluid leap through the air. I wasn't flying, and I hadn't yet located the Meeting Place, but I found the dreams immensely enjoyable.

We salute your newfound energy, commented the bear council. *This is what we mean by walking patiently, resolutely, like a polar bear. This has an 'authentic' ring to it and we feel your energies rise in relation to this. We are not worried about your abilities, Dawn; we chose you for a reason, just as you chose us. It was a match that serves to help, educate, and honor both of us, and more—all of us. It is a win-win-win situation, to use a human phrase.*

I continued to connect with Bering Strait and the Polar Bear

Council at least once a week. We spoke of many things—my progress in dreaming, Bering's life in the Arctic, and the council's ongoing discourse on a wide range of subjects.

Let us speak of the sky and the relation that polar bears have to the weather, they began one afternoon. *This is part of our medicine, one of our gifts, as it is for many animals. For polar bears it is especially relevant, not only to the connections between northern weather that is tethered or 'held' at the poles but also to planetary changes—or global warming, as you call it.*

Polar bears have always observed a direct relationship with the smell of weather—be it snow or ice, wind, clouds, or the qualities of air that are present as each weather occurrence moves through our land.

We have learned how to smell the shifting aspects of weather and so accommodate our actions to meet these changes in the best way, both for our survival and comfort. We are able to discern layers of potential change through the act of smell—many more than humans would guess. We offer you an experience to smell through polar bear nose and distinguish the variables.

What an intriguing proposal! Several animals had invited me to see through their eyes, even to feel through their bodies, but never had I received such a surprising invitation to discern layers of smell through a nose. I offered a tentative sniff.

I sensed the council laughing, assuring me that it is *"an acquired skill"* and that even polar bears need time and many experiences to fine-tune their abilities. However, they encouraged ongoing experimentation. *Not only will you begin to use your nostrils and olfactory senses in different ways, but your brain and sense organs will adapt to more finely discriminate and interpret the data.*

Polar bears have many, many generations of experience and accumulative knowledge to draw upon. We depend upon this to detect minute changes in snow, wind, sea, and ice; to locate seals and other prey; and to sense the presence of our allies, the Polar Bear spirits and sky friends.

Our sense of smell is also equated with who we are in our role as guard-

ians of the North. We sniff out anomalies. When something doesn't 'smell right,' polar bears come to attention. One observation we have for humans is that through your many technologies, factories, and altered scents you have lost much of your connection to this ancient art and science. You have been lulled into a basic 'good smell/bad smell' mentality, and have largely forgotten the subtle, but very revealing, language of smell.

Part of the polar bear 'dance' (as it is called by your researchers) is based on smell. We circle around each other to smell from all angles, to know if there is sickness, to learn where another bear has been and what experiences it has lived—all of this on the single hair of a polar bear!

We are also quick to clean ourselves. We do not like the scent of old blood or fat or other odors; it can be overpowering and distract us from our ability to smell others. We also maintain connections to our star friends via smell, though this is an ancient link, distinct and particular to polar bears.

New bears are first introduced to the language of smell within their mother's den. Each mother bear holds an experiential set of smells within her memory and conveys this to her young through dreams, encounters, and teachings. Birthing dens hold what humans might sense as an old, stale smell, but for bears it is a set of condensed smells, carefully gathered and layered. The odors of the den are a teaching environment offering an introduction to the basics of polar bear scents. These odors are a touchstone, helping young bears to learn quickly as they grow, as well as providing a reference so they may recognize certain smells and act wisely in future events. This is key to polar bear survival.

Cubs are brought back to the den soon after their first exposures to land and snow outside the den. The outside smells are both set within and compared against the polar bear den smell, which is the collective smell of polar bears at the most dense, enclosed level. It is essential for polar bear cubs to learn from smells, for each scent holds clues to favorable responses. The den holds the basic reference of this, a compendium of collective scents associated with past polar bear actions necessary for survival. Do you understand?

"I think you are saying that the den offers a 'smell key' for young bears to learn from and to use as a reference for future encounters. It's like a Big Book of Polar Bear Smells. Each scent in the book holds information, such as what it is and what actions may be best for bears to take on encountering that scent, based on the accumulated wisdom and experience of other bears. Is that it?"

That is close, not a bad comparison. We leave you with this image, as if you are a cub sniffing out new scents. And when you retreat to your human cave, perhaps you will find similarities with how humans do this in their way—not necessarily with smell (and yet that is there too). We look forward to hearing your experiences.

Yet another project?! But I thanked the bears and jotted down their idea in my own Big Book of Polar Bear Talks and Experiences.

SNIFFING DEEPER

Although I read many factual, research-oriented books about polar bears, I was also interested in the myths and legends that humans tell about bears. One of my favorites was about the mysterious polar bear men who walk upright during the day as polar bears and retire to remote igloos at night, taking off their skins to sleep as men.

One afternoon when the council asked for my questions, I proposed that we explore some of the quirky factoids humans have about polar bears. There were two I had in mind: first, that polar bears are left-handed and more likely to lead with their left side than their right; and second, an Inuit observation that polar bears cover their noses while hunting seals. I had read about both points in several books; sometimes they were conveyed as legends, other times as facts.

We appreciate your inquiries, began the council. *Questions such as these often lead to deeper explorations. This is why polar bears often put their noses to the snow or ice, to sniff out what might be—for even if it is nothing, it may lead to something else.*

To begin, not all polar bears are left-pawed. To understand more of this, however, you need to understand the kinesthetic awareness that polar bears use to relate to their environment, their geographical placement, their proximity to other bears, whether they are hunting or stalking, and their connection to the weather—so many variables!

Polar bears often lead with the left, this is true. We have a propensity to prefer walking counterclockwise around the pole, our left side to the pole, our right to the rest of the world. This connects with our walking dreams, for it is often easier for bears to flow into the dreamworld when moving from such a position.

When we walk with our left side to the pole, we are more likely to use our right paw in exploring the world, and when we walk with our right to the pole, we are more likely to use our left. This is our observation. Perhaps the humans who began the left-handed theory were simply meeting us from one fixed position. What do you think?

"I'm thinking there's probably something very telling beneath this observation."

What do you think it is?

"Well, in human symbology of the body, the left is often considered the unconscious side, while the right is the conscious side. In some Asian and Eastern countries, left-handed is gauche, considered awkward, wrong, or dirty, while the right hand is considered clean. Then again, the right side of the brain (which controls the left side of the body) tends to be more creative and intuitive, while the left (which controls the right side of the body) is more rational and logical. There are several human 'maps' of emotions and energies associated with different parts of the body."

Would it interest you to know that polar bears have similar maps? Ours are more about relationship to movement—about which paw goes first, which side of a polar bear better responds to mountains or water or, as mentioned previously, the pole.

One thing to keep in mind is that the pull of the magnetic north is much stronger in the Far North than where you live. And polar bears are more sensitive to this than humans—at least at this point in time.

(Formerly, humans were more sensitive and aware of the influences of such natural energies as well.) Thus, our maps are more about moving with the flow of natural energies.*

Sometimes we use our right paws and sometimes we use our left to swat at seals or whales or walrus. This depends on the situation and the unique confluence of energies.

However, the observation humans have about polar bears being left-handed may also derive from your understanding about our teaching or medicine. Perhaps we appear left-pawed to you because, from your perspective, we hold more unconscious energies—or more creative energies. Or, if you are frightened, then we appear more sinister—decidedly left-pawed. Do you see how that works?

"That's an interesting insight! And is this true for covering the nose as well?"

This is more of an urban legend as the phrase is used in human language, and yet some polar bears do cover their noses. There are times when we sense seals can see us, especially the darkness of our eyes and nose, and so this also has basis in reality, though perhaps not to the extent that humans have told this legend to others.

Let us set the record straight. We—the Polar Bear Council—are unique polar bears in that we have access to human knowledge about polar bears. Some humans reading this may wonder how we know these things. We remind you that we are dream spirits. As such, we can attune to the collective of human knowledge (including all your writings) about us.

At present time, much of your ancestral knowledge of us—as well as your deeper relationship to us—has been forgotten. There are only a few who remember the old ways, the old connections, and even that is wearing thin. So, we remind you that our group, this contingent, is here to bring forth more knowledge and remembering of who we are. We do this

---

*I later realized that humans also have maps that reveal natural energy flow—such as acupuncture diagrams illustrating the way *chi* (energy) travels through the body's meridians or, similarly, maps depicting subtle energy pathways in the Earth.

not simply to educate you about polar bears but to prompt you aware and awake into your own remembering of who you—humans—are as well.

We will stop for today. Bring your questions and we will continue our discussions. We remind you of your dream challenge to find the Meeting Place, and we welcome your participation.

With a fond, left-handed paw upon your shoulder,

The Polar Bear Council

11

Bar and Den

I found it unexpectedly. No seal hole, special aquarium, or dark puddle alerted me to its presence. I was leap flying along the dream road as I had every few nights for the past three weeks. Several times I had so enjoyed the gentle push-off of my foot followed by the high, smooth, graceful leap, that I lost focus, surrendering to the pleasure of rhythm and movement. But in this particular dream I was lucid, purposeful, allowing the momentum of the leap to propel me forward—and farther, I observed, than I usually traveled. I tingled as a buzz of energy shivered through my spine and I knew that the Meeting Place was near.

I stopped and surveyed. To my left I saw dark road, snowy trees, and jagged mountain tips gleaming white in the distance. Overhead, the black sky sparkled with stars. I noticed how clear the air seemed—sharp and bright, as if infused with crystalline clarity. In front of me, slightly to the right, was the narrow end of a lake. I knew this lake in waking life, having canoed along its perimeter several times. There should have been a shabby bar to the far right on a low rise, overlooking the lake, but in its place was an oblong, snow-domed structure. It looked like an elongated, puffed-up igloo with tiny porthole windows and an arched doorway.

With a few small leaps, I arrived at the door. It was made of wood, grayed and weather worn. A hand-polished walrus *oosik** served as door handle. Was this the entrance to the Meeting Place? Excited, anxious, curious, I placed my hand on the oosik, pulled open the door, and stepped inside.

The room was large, tidy, and dimly lit, with a U-shaped bar on the right, tables and booths to the left. Muffled sounds were followed by the slight hush that often happens when a stranger enters a sparsely crowded bar. I felt the flicker of eyes upon me, a momentary curiosity, and then more sounds—murmurs, shuffling feet (or paws?), the clack of glass against wood.

As the door closed behind me, I stood still, my eyes adjusting. The air felt warm, dense, and compressed, a contrast to the clean, moonlit clarity outside.

Now what? I wondered. I felt the push of nervous thoughts crowding my mind—Is this really the place? What should I do?—and reminded myself to center, to anchor my senses and stay lucid. Taking a deep breath, I was astonished by a sudden, rich intoxication of scents.

In a flash, I realized what the bears had tried to convey—there were layers of odors everywhere. All one needed to do was smell! How could I have not recognized that before? Lifting my nose, I sniffed in short bursts, each inhalation detecting a background medley of familiar scents—old beer, musty fabric, wood floors, crowded bodies—as well as odors I could not quite identify: a pungent tang like ripe, well-aged cheese; a warm saltiness that reminded me of puppy paws; a sharp, metallic odor like lightning on water.

Amazed at the range and precision of this newfound olfactory ability, wondering if it would translate to waking life, I gazed across the bar and was once again surprised. There was the familiar shape of Bering Strait. He stood upright against a dark, paneled wall. I raised my hand and he tilted his head in acknowledgment. Then, with a dramatic

---

*Baculum, or penis bone. Polished walrus oosik are sometimes used as door handles in Alaska.

flourish, he swooped his paw upward. A bright neon blue sign lit on the wall behind him:

WELCOME
TO THE
MEETING PLACE!

Ha ha, very funny, I thought. Touched by the great white bear's humor and laughing a little too hard, I woke myself from the dream.

CLUES AND PROPS

We applaud your creative spirit, commented the council during our next talk. I wasn't sure if they meant how I discovered the Meeting Place, that I envisioned it as an igloo-tavern, or that I managed a human sniff inspired by the Big Book of Polar Bear Smells. (Sadly, this ability did not work for me outside the dream. While I was now keen to sniff for scents and identify subtle odors, the dream experience was much more pronounced than anything I was able to accomplish in waking life.)

I visited the Meeting Place several more times, though each dream was different in focus and experience. I began to understand that the bar-igloo was my dreamworld version of a meeting place, the way my dream creators chose to portray the idea of this mutually accessible venue at this particular time.

For example, in one dream I discovered that each porthole window revealed a different landscape: the lake outside; a dark forest; a flat snowy expanse; some rugged mountains; and a churning, icy green sea. I took this to mean that shared dreamers come from near and far and, similarly, can travel anywhere. A meeting place is determined not by outer world geography but by common focus, intention, and resonance.

I saw different characters inside the bar as well—a group of bees immersed in telepathic conversation with a black bear, an old Native woman wrapped in caribou skins conferring with a female polar bear and her two cubs. And I observed some inventive ways that dreamers arrived and exited—through holes, trapdoors, and hidden portals. One of my favorites was a large, sharp-eyed raven swooping in through an impossibly small skylight in the ceiling.

The Polar Bear Council confirmed my understanding of the Meeting Place as a communal port of call, a dreamworld hub for like-minded dreamers to gather, a jumping-off point for shared dreaming to commence. Each dreamer may view the meeting place in his or her unique way, although advanced dreamers could design—through intention, repetition, and focused awareness—a shared setting to be experienced in the same way.

Your dream igloo-bar fits with our sense of self, as well as our purpose in opening to and meeting with both polar bears and humans throughout the ages, said the council. *We salute your creative ideas and will begin to add our own. Polar bears have a distinct vision and distinctive sense of humor, not always seen by humans. We feel you flowing wider, deeper with the creative spirit inherent in the telling of our tale. We lend our energies to your own.*

Bering Strait added his insights. My travels down the dark road were a human version of the polar bear dream walk. The flying leaps, he said, were my own twist, though bears, too, loved to fly and sail through the air in dreams. He confirmed my growing hunch that finding meeting places was a beginner's challenge. There were doorways in every dream, he agreed. Special aquariums, dark puddles, and snow igloos with oosik door handles—all these were props, personalized clues, invitations to further exploration, and reminders of what every dreamer already knows. So, too, can we create our own doorways to other places and shared experiences.

In one of my later dreams, I sat beside Bering Strait in a rounded booth, contemplating the concept of a meeting place as a blueprint, a shared idea, a mutually created space to converge and synchronize energies.

I was rapid-firing questions, trying to take advantage of our lucid connection and sum up what I had learned thus far: So, the Meeting Place is basically a collective template, and this igloo-bar is my perception of it? (*Yes.*) And there are as many versions of a meeting space as there are dreamers? (*Yes.*) But right now, in my version of the dream, you are seeing what I see? (*Yes.*) And yet you also have your own version of a meeting place? (*Yes, many.*) So, you see this igloo-bar as I see it because you are inside my dream, accessing and sharing my vision of it? (*Yes.*) How would it appear to you if you were not in my dream? If we were in your dream, how would this space appear to me? Can you show me how you see it?

With an exaggerated roll of the eyes, Bering Strait sighed.

DEN DREAMS

Pushing out of the booth, he sauntered on all fours toward the far right corner of the bar and I followed. A tunnel appeared in front of us, and in we walked, me crouching slightly. "In my dream, we are moving through a big hole in the wall," I told myself. "But what are we doing in his?" I wondered if we would cross a line, a boundary separating my dream vision from his. In the land of shared dreaming, where does one dreamer's perspective end and another's begin?

The tunnel opened to a round chamber, softly lit with bluish light from above. It felt safe and calm and peaceful. The walls had an icy sheen, and several seal skins were scattered on the densely packed, snowy ground. As I realized they were for me, I twinged with regret at how unaccommodating my dream space must have seemed to Bering—human-size booths, unsteady bar stools, no place for a big polar bear to relax!

He snorted softly. *To understand polar bear dreaming, we begin at the beginning.* Propping one skin against the wall behind me, I sat on another, and the great white bear began to share.

Imagine my birth in a den like this, a cave carved deep in a mountain of snow. My cub mate and I slip from the wet warmth of our mother's body into this strangely empty, open space. It is important we acclimate very quickly. This is an essential part of polar bear life—to feel at home in the dark cold of the cave, in the dark season of the polar night.

For many months, my sister and I nestle together, beside our mother, our senses adjusting, our bodies developing. Our mother dreams with us. This is not new to us, for even before our birth, we dreamed with our mother. She shares the stories of her life. We travel beside her in her dreams and are present in her memories, watching her adventures, surveying land, swimming through water, meeting other creatures, learning important things about becoming a polar bear.

When she dreams of walking through the dark polar night, our legs move as hers do; together, we travel in the dreamworld. Already we are imitating our mother, who will be our guide for several years. Although our eyes are closed and the cave is dark, we sense the silvery sheen of the outside world. We see many things through our mother's eyes: ice ridges, snow plains, open water—all these things we must learn about, as our mother instructs. We watch her smell the ice, catching scents upon the air, from the wind and snow and sea. We, too, can smell these things and learn even now—before encountering them—how to distinguish the scents of food and bears and strangers.

In other dreams, our mother shows us how to step upon frozen water, cautiously placing our paws, shifting our weight, testing for the fullness of a polar bear body. We understand this as a preview of things to come and watch with full attention.

In later dreams, our mother shows us how to move slow and silent, and when to charge and growl loudly. She shows us the proper way to greet other bears and share a feast of food. She will be our protector for some time, but we must watch her, do everything as she instructs. This is how we learn from her; this is her gift of teaching to us.

Soon it is time to go outside and experience these things for ourselves. It has been warm and safe inside the cave. Our love bond is very strong. Part of us wishes to remain here, like this; it is what we know. Our mother chuffs and tells us we will be happy to see many new things with our own eyes, to experience them for ourselves.

LIFE OUTSIDE

The first day we emerge from our den is like a second birth. We crawl up and out, scrambling onto white, bright snow! We sniff the air—our first teaching! It smells like nothing we know but holds hints of all the things we've learned. There is a fresh, open feel to the air that we have not yet experienced, for our cave air is close and warm, smelling mostly of bear. Everything here is new and bright and light!

We have seen visions of snow and ice and sky through our mother, but now it is all around us. Every direction we turn our heads is something new. My cub mate and I share feelings of wonder and excitement. As our mother reassures us, we bound into the snow. We push our faces into it—to smell it, taste it, know it. Snow will be our constant companion, with much information to share. We understand this is a time to play and learn—and, as our mother intimates, a time to learn through play.

We crawl and stretch and jump and run, spring and roll and turn and walk—all these actions we felt within the den, through our mother, through our dream bodies, are now alive in us! My cub mate and I are overjoyed with freedom and exaltation. These are human words, but they serve to describe some of our feelings. The pure joy of jumping into what we have dreamed about—now seeing, smelling, tasting, hearing, feeling, and knowing it for the first time—is a rare and delicious experience.

Our first visits outside the den are short but full. Our mother has learned from her previous cubs to bring us back soon. We tumble back into the dark warmth, nestling close to slumber. We absorb our experiences by settling all that we have learned within ourselves, inside our bodies, a foundation to our future dreams and adventures.

We leave the den for longer visits, each time finding something new. Our mother leads us over fluffy mounds, past jagged chunks of frozen snow, down slippery dips and hollows. She encourages us to know snow in different ways—to clean ourselves, to sleep upon, to hide behind, to smell and taste, to learn of food and danger. My sister and I watch and learn, then run and fall and tumble. When the air bites with cold, we run and huddle near our mother.

Inside the den, we suckle, sleep, and dream. We feel our mother growing restless. She shares a new dream: to take us down the mountain, to the ice and open water. We must also come to know the ice, to feel its movement beneath our paws, to listen when it speaks to us, to sense the coming weather. Once again, our mother shows us the animal that will provide our food: a fast, smart, skillful creature that holds delicious fat inside her body. She is called 'seal.'

Soon we will go to the ice. Our mother watches for changes outside our den, sniffing the snow and wind, smelling water and ice that lie far way. She encourages us to do this and we try. We do not always understand, but part of our learning is to imitate our mother. Whatever she does we try too, to learn from her.

Sometimes our mother shares dreams of her other cubs, those of several seasons past. There were two groups of cubs before us. The first time there was only one, a female who was her best student—so far. It is easier with one cub, our mother tells us. She does not mean this against us, but to share her knowledge, especially with my sister. The first female cub stayed with her for four full (yearly) seasons, beyond what is usually done, such was their connection. Then that cub went off to find her own way. Our mother is a smart bear, who has learned many things. We understand that she is respected by other bears, though we have yet to see these other bears. Soon enough, says our mother.

Her second litter was three cubs. She advises us—mostly my sister— that this is a difficult litter, for you must be strong to provide nourishment for three cubs. She shows us how she was overconfident with the birth of her first and how successful that cub turned out to be. It was not so with the second litter: two males and a female. One of the males was smaller than the others and not as fast. Our mother worked hard to help him, encouraging him to roll and tumble as his brother and sister, but this bear was not as agile. Still, they lived together for nearly a full season. They ate seal and swam and walked upon the ice and traveled far. Our mother taught the cubs many things. Still, at that time, in that place, the hunting was not so good, the small male was slow, and our mother knew he would not endure. She did not tell us all the story, though we felt her sadness when there were only two cubs left.

But, she tells us, two is a good number for cubs, male and female, so each can learn of the other. For in the seasons to come we will separate and go our own ways. Someday we will be as big and strong and smart as our mother.

Bering stopped with a gentle sigh. There was more, he said—leaving the cave, exploring the ice, learning to hunt, leaving his mother and sister, traveling alone, encountering other bears, finding a mate, meeting the council, and accepting a special assignment.

Enough for now, he said, and we sat still for several moments, silently sharing the dream.

12

Becoming Polar Bear

As our talks progressed, I noticed myself becoming more accepting, opening more wholeheartedly to the fluid, circular manner Bering Strait and the Polar Bear Council directed their requests and handled their responses.

I had asked Bering how he saw the Meeting Place from his perspective, and he answered by sharing memories of his birth and the influence of dreaming from an early age. It wasn't a reply that made perfect human sense, yet the experience of deepening and participating in Bering's world seemed more and more an essential part of polar bear teaching.

We feel you touch our heart, commented the Polar Bear Council. *Our perceptions are more readily available to you for seeing and feeling inside your being. You, too, are a polar bear person, a polar bear dreamer, and you are opening deeper to our message, understanding the importance of telling our story to others. For this we are happy and grateful and honored to share.*

READY FOR ADVENTURE

The last time I saw my version of the Meeting Place, I awoke in the dreamworld a short distance from the igloo-bar.

Bering Strait stands upright, casually leaning one shoulder against the door, front paws crossed, as if waiting for me. He wears a jaunty, navy blue cap. As I approach, he asks if I am ready for an adventure. I laugh. Does he really think I'd have any other answer than Yes!?

Together, we head toward the lake. There is no snow or ice, but as usual, it is late at night. Moonlight shimmers in silvery ripples upon the water. A gathering of bears mingles on the shore. Like Bering, they stand and walk upright. They are smaller than normal bears, their features and gestures humanlike. Some wear clothes—bright sky blue pants, ornate vests of deep red and gold. White paper globes, lit from within, hang from tree branches and sway in the breeze, glowing like bright, happy moons. The colors, movements, and jovial way the bears interact with each other make the setting festive and welcoming.

With a tilt of his nose, Bering directs my vision to a cord strung between two trees. Spaced evenly along the cord are hangers, holding what look to be bulky garments. As I move closer, I see they are bear costumes of different shapes, sizes, and colors. A young, female polar bear–human, perhaps a teenager—slight in build, with long, silky white hair, a furry human face, and distinct polar bear nose—holds out a costume for me. I shake my head, no thanks, and take a step back, but Polar Bear Girl is insistent, pushing the outfit my way.

I look to Bering and he nods, *Try it on.*

Holding the garment, I feel my resistance to this game. The fuzzy white outfit seems silly, like a child's costume. Probably made in China, I think dismissively. Polar Bear Girl snorts and taps one brightly polished claw on a label at the collar: *"Handcrafted in Germany."*

Reassured by the label, encouraged by Bering and the young female bear, I step into the suit. It fits loosely but now that I have it on, I note some impressive details: the paws are thickly padded, covered with toughened skin and sharp claws that feel remarkably real; the coarse fur varies in length, texture, and color (clear, white, ivory, yellow) on different parts of the body. Once I have both legs and arms tucked within the suit, Polar Bear Girl reveals the head of the costume: a big bobble contraption with two small rounded ears, a large muzzle, and circular holes for eyes.

She sets the head atop my neck. It's bulky and top-heavy, and I balk at once. There is no way I can comfortably move with this balanced on my shoulders. I start to protest, but then a strange thing happens.

I feel the suit shrinking, contracting closer to my skin, as if being vacuum sealed against my body. At the same time, I feel my body expanding, my muscles becoming denser and thicker, bulking up and out, filling the suit. I can feel the bobble head conforming to my head, which is simultaneously reshaping itself, elongating and thickening. The sensation of my body inflating and the costume skin shrinking, the two layers meeting and fusing together, is strangely pleasant, not at all uncomfortable. I glance at Bering, who is carefully watching my transformation.

My body tips forward to a more natural all-fours position. I am suddenly aware of exquisite sensitivity in my front paws—a kind of springiness, as if I can feel *into* the ground, at least several inches down. I take a few tentative steps, testing the spongy feeling of polar bear paws sinking into the earth. It's an odd sensation, for I can feel the paw pads physically touching the ground as well as energetically touching beneath the surface—an unexpected extension of feeling.

Suddenly, Bering charges forward—amazingly fast!—racing to the shore, splashing exuberantly into the water. Without a thought, I bolt, my body shooting forward from my hind legs—such power!—as I chase the big white bear.

As soon as my body hits the water I am again surprised with sensation—this time, a feeling of pressure and buoyancy. My senses are attuned in a new and different way, and I am aware of a layer of tiny bubbles all around me, in the spaces between the hairs of my fur. I am conscious of the dense, cushiony layer of fat supporting my body as it bobs in the water. I wonder if this is what it is like for all polar bears or just the way I feel, as a human inside a polar bear body, inside a dream.

How easy my front legs paddle forward, and how strong my back legs and open paws propel me through the water! It is a satisfying sensation—much easier than human swimming!—and I understand why polar bears feel at home in the water. Ahead of me, the rounded shape of Bering's back and shoulders gleam pearly white against the dark moonlit water. Then—he plunges. I wait for him to reappear but already I know that I, too, must plunge. With a quick breath, I lower my head and arch my body. A few strong, clean kicks—how amazingly streamlined I feel in the water!—and I'm diving down.

All is dark, nothing to see, but farther down we go. Down, down, until at last we are coming up! It's not that we have changed directions; rather, down has suddenly become up. The water has changed as well. It feels dense and silky. Popping my head upward, surfacing above the waterline, I see we are in a different place. The same bright black sky, brilliant moon and stars loom overhead, but the smooth dark water is punctuated with white chunks of jagged ice. In front of us there is a long, sloping, snowy shore.

Bering hauls up and out of the water and I paddle toward him, dodging the ice chunks, some of which are quite huge. Everything seems very sharp and clear. What I thought was the shore is actually a floe, a long floating sheet of snow-covered ice. Placing my front paws flat upon its surface, I kick my hind legs to push my body upward. But it's not as easy as it seems, and down I splash. I try again, this time reaching forward, pulling up, and pushing out, my big wet body drizzling and dripping upon the snow.

The shake is automatic: a shiver that begins in the head and neck, unleashing a shimmy of energy down shoulders, legs, and bum. It's an interesting sensation—the power of the shake causing the outer layers of skin and fur to jiggle loose and rotate rapidly around the body, flinging water outward, ever faster at the extremes. What a clever trick! I think, now knowing exactly how it is done through the feelings of this body.

And now I'm dry. Bering makes a show of diving forward onto a fluffy mound, twisting and turning to rub his face, neck, belly, back, and sides into the snow. *Dry cleaning,* he remarks as he deftly rights himself and shakes once again. I laugh and notice the jaunty, blue cap tossed upon the ice—had it really survived that dive and swim?

A memory marker, Bering says.

"What?"

You'll see.

We climb a small rise and sit against a curved ridge of snow. Thin streaks of green and red sway gracefully against the starry sky. Shiny chunks of ice wobble in the dark water before us.

Listen, says Bering.

I hear our breath and the sounds our bodies make as they rest upon the snow. I hear tiny wavelets of water lapping against ice and the crinkling, static song of the aurora above. I hear deep water moving below us, the distant groan of ice, and a delicate skittering of wind across crusted snow.

Just as I once smelled layers of scent in the igloo-bar, I now hear layers of sound. Everything has a unique tone that is also a feeling, a resonance that speaks to us, through us. I am aware of a larger range and depth of sound waves, as if my body has awakened to feel sound—not just inside my head but through vibrations playing upon the hairs of my body, through my paws and face and ears. All around, the Arctic world is *speaking* to me.

I know I am dreaming. But so also am I here, present in the dream in a new way. I feel my very being fusing into the landscape, connecting with sky and snow and water, a dreamer awake within the Arctic. I am filled, happy and content, but tired too. Sitting beside Bering Strait, I am aware of the immense energy polar bears must possess, not simply to survive, but to live and dream as they do.

THE PRESENCE OF NOW

The dream of becoming a polar bear wrapped itself around me for several days. It was a wonderful dream, and I felt calm and centered—and changed. I noticed sounds and smells with deepened, renewed appreciation; I was aware of the way the soles of my feet pressed lightly into the ground.

A few days after the dream, while shopping in the grocery store, an elderly, white-haired gentleman stood beside me in the produce section. As I reached for an orange, he bumped me with his elbow. I turned to smile at him, to let him know it was okay, and he smiled back. It was one of those smiles that lights up a face. He had beautiful, bright blue eyes and a jaunty, navy-blue cap upon his head. *The memory marker.*

"I like your hat!" I exclaimed, pointing to his head, laughing a little too loud and long. I hoped I wasn't scaring him, but immediately he joined in, laughing graciously, exuberantly. And there we stood in front of the navel oranges, side by side, laughing, sharing a simple, deep-rooted joy.

We will tell you a story about dreaming and our connection with humans, the Polar Bear Council said later that day. I had asked them about the memory marker, explaining how a jaunty, blue hat showed up both in the dreamworld and in waking life. I wondered if Bering's hat had caused me to notice the one the elderly man wore in the grocery store, or perhaps the one I observed in the grocery store had inspired what appeared in the dream. It was an odd thought, I knew, but the idea of awakening to future thoughts and memories in the past suddenly seemed just as likely as recalling past thoughts and memories in the future. I likened it to the bear suit compressing against me as my body bulked up to meet it. The power of transformation was in the middle.

This is the story you need to hear, confirmed the council. *It is a story of direction, a long-distance map of where we came from, where we are headed, and all points between. Past and future—these constraints of time are human in many ways. Our dreaming leads both into the future and into the past and pulls them round to each other, inside ourselves, in the presence of now. Let us begin.*

There was once a woman who dreamed of polar bear people. She was awake to the ways of polar bears—not so much at first, but the polar bear people called to her spirit in her dreams as she wandered through Arctic lands, opening her eyes and heart to the larger, deeper ways of polar bears.

She learned to walk slowly, to stop and see and listen and feel—not just with her eyes and ears but with her whole being. That in itself is a teaching for a lifetime! That is a return of wholeness to humanity, a gift from all animals, an opening to the fullness of planet Earth and beyond.

This woman felt the heart song of the polar bear. By dreaming, she opened a door that had been closed. By waking up, she remembered that she too was a polar bear spirit. In this way she helped others find a dream track between human and polar bear dreamers.

Things are both more and less than what they seem upon this Earth. A new vision is needed for planetary consciousness to awaken, and that vision begins inside, in calm darkness, such as might be found in a polar bear den. It begins with the dreaming of a mother bear to her cubs, a mother planet to her children. As the cubs adjust to the dream in the den, within themselves, they bring new life to the world. And that is what this story is about: the coming alive of humanity, in a new way, with a new vision, and with new hope for the United Planet of Beings.

13
The Human-Polar Bear Alliance

My dreams returned to the Arctic, walking beside Bering Strait. It was not so different from the seed dreams—that peaceful, purposeful walking, side by side, through the vast, white expanse. And yet, so much had changed. I felt settled, not only within the dreams, but within myself.

I often saw the council's snow cave hovering on the horizon, a small dream icon reminding me of their presence. I was more aware of the seamless connection between Bering and the council. Sometimes while speaking with the lone polar bear, I sensed the old polar bear spirits listening.

Greetings from the Polar Bear Contingent and the wild world of Bering Strait! they began enthusiastically one morning as I sat before my desk.

We acknowledge and celebrate Bering Strait as a real polar bear living in the Arctic as well as a member of our council. He wears many hats: dreamer, detective, interpreter, and instigator. We say this with some humor because we are happy to share with him, with you, with all bears and humans, in many varied ways.

The more you connect with us in dreams and participate in sharing thoughts, the more deeply we merge our consciousness with yours. Together, we facilitate an opening between our species. This is our agenda. Many animals all over the world are similarly working with groups of humans and individuals such as yourself. Our goal is to create a bridge of conscious-ness with humans, to reawaken a way of being in which all share and learn from each other via the universal language of being.

Polar bears have a unique teaching in this regard. We travel great distances—not only in the physical world. More than many animals, polar bears are bridgers between worlds. We link the deeper earth with the sur-face of the land, the land with water, the water with sky and stars. We bridge above and below, energies from the top of the world with the entire planet. Merging our consciousness with snow and ice, sea and sky, we know our environment intimately.

We are also consciously connected with humans. This may seem a par-adox since we are not often in contact with humans via physical encoun-ters. And yet, there is a good reason for this. Do you want to take a guess?

I pondered. "Perhaps because you are so geographically distant from most human populations, you can see us more clearly? And maybe because you are removed from our ordinary lives, we project less upon you? That is, we don't live with polar bears as we do with dogs or cats, so we don't really know you as individuals, but more as a concept—wild polar bears wandering around the North Pole."

This is an interesting attempt at understanding. Our connection with humans is limited by distance, generally removed from physical contact, that is true. And there is less personal projection on polar bears than on dogs or cats, your prime pets. Yet, you have a good deal of projection on polar bears. Humans are great projectors!

Our original alliance derives from an older time when polar bears enjoyed a special relationship with humans who lived in the high Arctic. A promise was involved. Polar bears provided humans with meat and skin and teaching, and humans agreed to work with us in the dreamworld con-structing a pathway linking the deep earth to the stars. This was to be a joint venture, a coming together of two species in a creative way. It was a means of participating in a larger presence of consciousness that united humans and polar bears, working together to make a dream path visible. That is part of our sacred trust with Gaia—our 'assignment' to connect the stars, lower earth, and waters. The whales are involved in this as well, though polar bears are the primary bridgers between the land and sea in this regard.

Perhaps you will dream of links between sea and ice, land and water, or Earth and stars, and tell us what you experience. We leave you in the spirit of co-creative adventure, with kind regards.

LARGER VEHICLES OF AWARENESS

For me, assignments from the Polar Bear Council were both intriguing and frustrating. While their suggestions usually led to impressive experiences in the dreamworld, I often felt confused afterward, unable to quite make out how the experience fit within the overall scheme of polar bear teaching. Understanding required patience and deepening.

That night, with aim to follow the council's suggestion, I dreamed of the Arctic once again. I was not walking, but gliding in a prone position, skimming over an immense ice field that glistened silver white with moonlight. Bering was beside me. Our movement was smooth and graceful. I wasn't directing the movement, and yet I felt myself as an essential component of its fluid motion. I sensed the Polar Bear Council's presence infusing my body, opening me to the environment. We were all connected—Bering, me, the council, the land and sea and sky. Thus I flowed in an expansive, pleasurable current of energy and spirit, sailing low over the bright icy landscape.

At one point I glanced back and saw two figures following a short distance behind. With a start of amusement, I realized it was Bering Strait and me. Our gait was calm and steady, nothing out of the ordinary. Yet seeing myself there—and feeling myself here—I suddenly understood a key aspect of polar bear dreaming: the dream walk!

Bering mentioned this ability several times, but I didn't fully grok it until this moment. We had bilocated ourselves in the dreamworld. That is, we were both walking through the dream landscape and extending our consciousness ahead of us.

For me, this was extraordinary enough, but Bering asserted that polar bears can do this while waking—moving their physical body through the real Arctic as their dream self projects forward, into the distance, or into the future! What a marvelous ability: to preview obstacles and seek out alternate routes, to discern tomorrow's weather patterns, to know when to forge on and when to retreat.

"Whoa!" I exclaimed to Bering, who snorted softly and zoomed ahead.

We are pleased you have expanded your sensory abilities, that you have 'come on board' to feel into the polar bear way of traveling through the worlds, began the Polar Bear Council the following morning.

Our connection with humans in attempting to co-create a larger vehicle of awareness has occurred several times during our mutual history. There were periods when many humans were open and we worked together in this way, along with other animal spirits. There were also times when humans were shut down and we communicated with only a few in the dreamworld.

Our dream interface with humans often happens through walking side by side. This is a central action in your dreams, and for very good reason. Polar bears walk. We do our best connecting while walking. For us, the physical act of walking is a means of aligning ourselves with earth lines— what you might call meridians of the planet's body—and, through that, deepening our connection with the spirit of Earth.

This connection is the missing link when you ask why or how humans separated from conscious participation in the web of life and the universal language. For humans, there was a moving away from that connection with Earth as mother. Some animals feel humans are still in this rebellious phase, not learning—or refusing to learn—from their mother and failing to appreciate the wisdom she shares freely with all.

But humans had another task in mind, and many animals supported your species in the desire to break away and come to know yourselves in a new way. Polar bears are one of these animal groups, especially in regard to dreaming. The same is true of whales and dolphins in our area.

We reenter collective human consciousness on a larger scale at this time to offer a new perspective: the patient hunting of deep self. Polar bears are masters at this because we live in a deep and often solitary connection with the Earth. Our diversions are fewer than many animals. We work with whales and seals, with some birds and plants, and with sky and ice, water and snow. And with our beloved star connection, which is the next bridge for humans to make as well.

But understand that humans must first remember their connection with Earth. It is what you might call a 'do-not-pass-go' type of remembering that has yet to be fully awakened, to be deeply felt by all humans. Mother Earth trembles and shakes and tries to awaken you, but humans are stuck in their own denial and rebellious nature.

Polar bears are patient animals. Thus, we have the task to walk beside you—to remind you, gently, persistently, patiently, of your deeper connection. Do you understand?

I nodded.

In order to write this book, to share our wisdom with the human people, you, too, need to be able to bridge. Bridging the pathways from waking to dreaming is one such challenge.

THE ORIGIN OF THE COUNCIL

Let us begin with a story, said the council several days later. As was often the case, the flow of our conversation followed a circuitous route, spiraling round to pick up threads once discussed and visit them anew. I had grown to appreciate this trait, this polar bear quality of sniffing out treasure, investigating side roads, examining a curiosity from many different points of view.

Once upon a time, all beings were united in common song. This is not a fanciful way of referring to this time period, for this is exactly what it was. In those early days, both polar bears and humans were attuned to the waking dreamworld. Our relationship was one of give and take, borrow and share. This was the typical gesture of all beings participating in the One, supportive of the collective good of all.

Some humans were especially intrigued by polar bears, for our teaching was considered specialized. We worked primarily with shamans, or powerful dreamers of the North—Siberian, Inuit, Inupiat, and more. But we also worked with dreamers from other lands. Our connections went far and wide, not limited to the northern climes. We are not always seen as polar bears—some see us as Northern spirits or as dancing lights in the sky (which, incidentally, is why polar bears are often pictured in whimsical drawings as dancing, for there is a dance to our movement and our being).

The Polar Bear Council was founded to maintain the connection between polar bears and humans in light of planetary evolution. In human Earth years, the council was founded approximately three hundred years ago. Before that time there were still many viable connections, as well as a self-appointed group of spirit beings who held the connection between polar bears and humans in the dreamworld.

The council was initially formed of spirit bears as well as physical polar bears adept at dreaming. All polar bears see within the dreamworld while waking, but some polar bears have a greater aptitude. They are more drawn to their dreaming abilities. Because they focus upon and use these abilities, they are simply better at it than others. This is similarly the case for humans.

In the time frame mentioned, some three hundred human years ago, many polar bears needed help and guidance as their dreaming abilities were severely shocked by a sudden change in our relationship with humans. There was a falling away of the ties that had been present between us. This occurred during the 'Whale Wars,' when many polar bears were killed or taken away to far-off lands—not for meat or skin or a desire to learn but from human fear, bravado, and a desire to dominate.

Before this event, we enjoyed a relationship with humans based on trust and mutual respect. When that was compromised, there was a soul shock to the Polar Bear people, and many broke off their dreaming abilities with the humans. That is, our dreaming became closed to humans. Some polar bears also closed dreaming within themselves.

During this time the Polar Bear spirit guides intervened and offered the idea of a council to help physical polar bears remember their ties to the dreamworld and their promise in relationship to humans. The council would help mentor and encourage living polar bears in their abilities to dream and, in some cases, link them with humans who were similarly inclined to dream large.

We exist now—as then—to support and guide polar bears who are open to dreaming, to oversee polar bear and human dreamers as teams, and to encourage the human–polar bear remembering.

Our vision was initially to restore the balance of humans and polar bears to mutual respect and trust. However, the Earth is changing more quickly than expected, and we now sense the need for a new, more open alliance than occurred in the past.

This is exciting, yet it has potential pitfalls. As mentioned, we feel it is the human animal who is endangered. Polar bears will continue in our form, whether on this planet or in other dimensional worlds. Because the human animal has this world as its primary base, your species seems to teeter at an all-or-nothing point.

We desire to reassure and tell you again that many animal species are working with humans at this time—as are nature spirits, star energies, spiritual guides, and the Earth herself, including the people of the lower earths and waters. Great assistance is available.

Many humans have stumbled into apathy; many slumber in superficial ways that divert their attention from the depths of who they really are. It is ironic that so many humans project that animals are 'dumb' when what is most obvious to all of us—the creatures of planet Earth—is so often unseen by your species. This is not to make light or point paws or fingers in blame but simply to indicate that many humans run wild with self-projection.

The Polar Bear people offer healing wisdom for humans at this time.

We are about moving slowly, resolutely, patiently through the vast frozen world of one's soul. This is not a recommendation to change your soul's journey, but to see it as it is, to see the beauty of this path, this choice—not to divert, but to embrace the furthest edge of who you have become and move beyond, to remember yourself with the dance of all creation.

Do you have any questions?

Plenty, I thought. I was thinking mostly of the "soul shock" that polar bears experienced during the Whale Wars, as the council termed it. I had read about events occurring in the Arctic during the 1700s and 1800s, when early European explorers and whalers encountered the great white bears.[1] Prior to this point, polar bears were considered a wonder, a majestic, mythlike creature due to their impressive size, coloring, and icy habitat. Unfortunately for the bears, however, whalers reacted poorly to first contact. What was often simple curiosity and a desire to investigate human activity on the part of polar bears was interpreted as aggression on the part of whalers. Exercising "self-defense" against the bears soon became an excuse to capture, cage, torment, lance, skin, behead, and kill. Whalers brought exaggerated tales and claims of combat with the fierce, monstrous white beasts back to the "civilized" world. It is easy to see how the roots of our projections upon polar bears as ferocious man-eaters thus took hold.

"I'm curious about how our mutual dreaming was closed during those Whale Wars," I began. "Did that occur because of what the humans did? Or did the humans behave as they did because their dreaming was already closed off?

"Second, about the polar bear wisdom you mentioned at the end—about moving slowly through 'the vast frozen world of your soul.' Can you elaborate on that?"

These questions are connected in a meaningful way, and it is no mistake that you ask about them together.

In answer to your first question, it is both ways that you propose—and more. The humans who killed were closed off from their dreaming or they would not have acted in such an unthinking, unfeeling way—to take so brazenly, without asking. Such actions speak of a disconnected soul. The desire to assert power and control was a reaction to this loss of connection. And yes also, because of these actions the dreaming was cut off. The two halves involve each other—it is similar to your human question of "Which came first, the chicken or the egg?" In some ways it is a pointless question, and yet, it is a step into seeing who you are and how these actions influence who you will become.

Humans chose a path of moving away from conscious connection with all life. That is not necessarily bad or misguided. Rather, let us see it as an exploration of how far one species can move into forgetting, and to discover what links remain to remembering. The answer is that both exist—both the forgetting and the remembering, though on different levels or states of being.

Humans, as polar bears and all beings, are multidimensional souls. As such there is always the opening to explore many options, many ways of being. Humans are a unique group (though, of course, all species are unique!) in that they have evolved many diversions at the expense of being conscious of their inherent connection with All That Is. Some humans retain this memory—all humans do at deep levels, though some humans also hold this knowing consciously.

Where does this take us, you wonder. It takes us back to the movement of walking across the vast, frozen world of your soul, which is to say the place that humans have wandered into and have chosen to tread upon for further, deeper exploration. Humanity is at a precipice of being—a dangerous yet exciting point at which to evolve or perish. Many other species have reached this point; some disappear from the Earth, others adapt and evolve. It is always a choice.

Humans have an extensive, interconnected set of stories (myths, belief systems, scientific paradigms, religious paradigms, and so forth). You might think of this as a vast net holding yourselves in the illusion of who you think you are. The call of many animals is to help you release this net, to realize it is a net of your own making.

We are polar bears. In many ways we are simple creatures. We walk and hold the earth together with the sky and lower waters. We listen to the whales, our friends, and we eat seals, our partners in the dance of life becoming. We nurture our greater family by offering dreams to our children and to the dreaming bears who work to hold the earth together.

There is so much that humans are not aware of. All animals hold an energetic task of healing or awakening—a specialized medicine for others upon the Earth. Without that species, there is necessary change and mutation.

Without polar bears, you are sunk in a big way. Polar bears are big beings who offer big dreaming to all the world, especially to humanity at this time.

What we offer is a slowing down, a deepening, a clearer vision of where you are in your own evolution. Perhaps you are so fearful of who you have become that you do not wish to see, and so you jump into endless diversions.

We offer you a larger way of seeing your true being and an entreaty to embrace that being as you accept the fullness of who you really are.

We are the Polar Bear Council and we offer you our paw in collective dreaming, so that you may open yourself on wider levels to the majesty of what we—all creatures of the Earth and beyond—have created. We welcome you to the party.

14
Bridge of Dreams

We zigzag through choppy ice chunks and jagged snow drifts. Simultaneously, we zoom ahead, our outstretched bodies passing low over dark, open water, tiny waves rippling silver gray with moonlight.

Bering encouraged me to shift focus between my dream body and its extension of consciousness as we continued playing with the dream-walk technique. I understood this as yet another way of bridging perspectives, transitioning my viewpoint from a walking position to a floating extension of vision. In the beginning, I was only able to see from one perspective, but the more we played, the more I was able to maintain dual awareness. We also began soaring upward, lifting our consciousness skyward as we walked. Bering indicated this was a taste of how some polar bears sailed into communion with the star people, as they simultaneously dream walked through the Arctic night.

I recognized how so many of my polar bear dreams were part of a larger teaching, a progressive study of different dream tasks: finding dream locales, meeting other lucid dreamers, sharing consciousness, shifting form, merging thoughts, seeing through the eyes of another. I accepted this twilight zone quality of the bears' Arctic dreamworld in which all was permeable, open to exploration and relationship.

In one lucid dream in which we weren't doing anything particularly fancy, just walking and conversing, Bering proposed a special meeting. I was curious and about to ask questions—What kind of meeting? With whom, or what?—when he nodded to a small mound on the ice field ahead. As we approached I saw the mound was a sleeping female polar bear, huddled low in a snow bed.

She seemed very, very old—frail and ancient. Was she even alive? Perhaps she was present in the dreamworld simply as a marker to the past. But then her eyes opened; they were deep, dark wells that seemed to embrace and invite—portals to distant times? different worlds? My heart warmed as I felt her spirit connect with mine.

In the background, Bering announced, *Now shifting temporal dimensions!* I wanted to laugh but was too fascinated by how my dream body was expanding and diffusing. I felt hyperaware, sensing all of my molecules speeding outward. At a certain point, I lost track of myself. But then, there I was—sitting in a snow drift between the two bears.

The three of us watched a review of the female bear's life. To me, it appeared as an old black-and-white film. The female bear seemed to have the remote control, pausing briefly at special points of interest: her cubs, her travels, and a series of encounters in which she discovered her purpose.

Unlike Bering, her forte was not dreaming but remembering. Just as Bering Strait was a living link to the Polar Bear Council, this bear held connections to the ancestral world, to the living memories of polar bear history. At one point I turned to glance at her and saw long crystals of light, like shards of ice infused with brilliance, emanate from her body. I felt I was in the presence of a very wise, loving, and generous being.

She proposed sharing memories of the schism between polar bears and humans, and I felt my thoughts merge with hers. Together, we remembered; from a high perspective, we watched small groups of humans trek across the frozen Bering Sea. I felt their fears, their physical pangs of cold and hunger, and underlying excitement, too—a determination to press on, to find home in this frozen world. In the beginning, the humans were wary, keeping their distance as the bears watched, intrigued by the scent of this new arrival.

In time we met the human peoples, and they met us, related a voice from the past, perhaps an ancestor bear recalling how life once was. *Such puny bodies they had, not much strength, and yet they were similar to us in some ways—curious, resourceful, strong in spirit.*

We became their teachers, showing them by example how to recognize breathing holes and birthing lairs, when to wait and when to strike, and how to pull a grown seal with one heave upon the ice. We taught them to converse with waves and wind, to smell the coming snow so as to know when to retreat and when to hunt. From us, they learned to spread their limbs upon thin ice, so as to travel safely across frozen water.

There was sharing in our relationship, respect and honor as well. When the hunters called to us so their people could live, we provided skin and fur for warmth and protection, flesh and fat for nourishment, and more.

All over the North, humans called to us with earnest voice: 'Oh, Nanook, come to us.' Then all the village would partake of polar bear, eating our body, wearing our fur. Sometimes a bear would eat a hunter, and so we knew of each other in this way too. A doorway opened between our beings, and the spirit of life flowed between us.

The humans told stories about us, made carvings and wore our bones, cleaned and polished and revered our skulls. Our skins were not only warm coverings, but reminders of powerful Bear Medicine. 'Slip into our skin and feel through our body,' we called to those who listened and watched, to those who desired to dream journey with us.

Some followed our tutelage, joining us in the dreamworld. Some explored with us, journeying to other realms. And some worked beside us, helping create pathways to the lower earth and sky. Working with those humans, we too learned new ways of being.

Some related to us in spirit, others in more physical ways. But even those who did not participate recognized the open doorway between us. Our skins were well tended and honored, our flesh not eaten without first giving thanks, for the peoples of this time saw our spirits just as they saw their own ancestors. They knew what was right and how to talk with the departed, to encourage their souls to return so the cycle of life might continue.

For many ages we communed with humans in this way. They told stories of our kind, praising our teachings, recounting the visions we shared with shamans. We, too, related stories of our encounters with humans. Our stories intertwined, nourishing each other as it was done in those days, when a human could be a bear, or a bear a human, and it made no real difference—for a soul, once departed from its body, was free to choose how to live its next life.

Then a different kind of human arrived—takers from the sea. They plunged spears into the first of us who came to investigate, ever inquisitive as is our nature. They killed females with cubs, our young, and, mostly, the largest among us. They skinned our bodies still warm with life, not asking for our blessing, no sense of honor, not appreciating anything we had to teach, only taking, taking.

Our spirits lumbered round their floating dens that stunk of greed. We found their hearts small and hard, their eyes glazed with something we could not comprehend. The more resentful among us led some of them into icebergs and arctic mists, to freeze or drown or disappear, but it was not enough. This was a time of spirit forgetting, a maligning of the open heart path between us.

We went away from the humans, not with our bodies but with our minds and spirits. We holed up inside ourselves, among our own kind. We walked the light lines of the earth, holding together the top of the world, because this is what we do. Even when others do not participate in the dance of balance, we hold our light.

In time the takers went away. But other humans came. Some killed us and dragged our bodies to far-off lands. Some watched from a distance and tried to learn from us, but their heart vision was closed, believing that to watch us with human eyes was to know us. Still others came from the sky. They chased us noisily from above, spearing us from long weapons that left us sleeping or frozen in all our limbs. These were strange, mad men, pulling plugs of skin from our hide, sapping blood and milk and fluids from our bodies, stealing—claws, teeth, fur—and chattering with self-congratulations in their camps how none of us were harmed.

There are always a few humans who are different. In every age this is so. Some remember and honor the bond we once shared. We do not know if humans will accomplish their task. That is up to you. We draw upon our ancient medicine, the bridge of dreams, to connect our hearts to yours.

SOLE TO SOUL

The experience of meeting the female polar bear stayed with me for many days. Although several research books I read offered a short nod to ancient human–polar bear ties, it seemed obvious that we generally fail to acknowledge the vital importance of the early relationship between humans and polar bears.

As bridgers of the Far North, polar bears hold a very special medicine for our planet. It seems we have largely forgotten what the ancient Arctic people once knew and honored about the bears. Masters of dream exploration, adventurers of extremes, wisdom linkers of land and sea and sky, polar bears are strong spirit helpers. Sensitive to the Earth's meridians, their keen adaptability, introspection, and connection with Spirit allow them to traverse barren lands, windswept ice fields, and frozen seas, not only to survive but to thrive. It was Polar Bear that Arctic shamans consulted for their most important visions. What would happen if we lost this connection completely?

Let us begin, together, with how you hold the sole of your soul upon the planet, the Polar Bear Council said a few days later. *This is one of the most elemental polar bear teachings. As you know, we move with conscious connection. Polar bears have sensitive paws (and pause) with regard to the earth. We tread upon land, snow, and ice; we swim through water. We are at home in our skins and in the way we move through different mediums.*

This is an important teaching we bring to the human people during this period of transition.

We offer an opening of soul to sole—what you might call the collective soul to your sole connection with the earth. This ties into our role as bridgers, especially between the peoples of the lower earth with the surface. Humans are often called the surface people by some animal groups. This is because you walk upon the surface of the earth and because your consciousness is often focused in a superficial, surface way.

Sole and soul, paws and pause—for a moment I smiled, amused as always by the bear's play on language, rich with pun and double entendre. It occurred to me, however, that I was also proving their point, allowing my thoughts to skitter on a veneer of humor.

As you note, interjected the council, *many messages, terms, and phrases from animals are multiple with meaning. This is true of life as well. And, we would add—the deeper and more expansive your consciousness, the greater access you have to these multiple layers of meaning.*

Back to our movements: polar bears move swiftly, yet not hurriedly, upon the ice and land. We are most at home on the frozen ocean; this is partly due to our search for food but also because we have an affinity with the people of the lower waters, as well as the whales.

Both northern whales and polar bears share a similar soul shock from humans; we have a closeness in that regard. We share information with the whales and they with us. The whales travel farther than we do and have a different type of job, but they honor our role as holders of the pole, just as we honor their roles as they 'sing' or sound tones that bring star energies to Earth.

We also bring a special energy to the Earth. This was not something we originally signed on for, but these things occur—new plans develop as you are holding old ones. This is true for humans, as well as many other animal groups, right now.

We hear the call of spirit to join all the unique energies of Earth. We are bridgers, so we can help. We are all part of planetary evolution, for it is something of an all-or-nothing movement. That is why you may hear that some animals are like bodhisattvas, for many have done their time, completed their evolutionary requirements, but stay on the Earth to help others advance. You will see this more and more, not only with individual animals (including humans) and animal groups, but with nature spirits and guides from many different aspects of existence. The advancement of Earth—the full flowering of planet Gaia—is dependent upon the blossoming consciousness of all.

Do you have any questions?

"What is the key message you would like to tell humans in this regard?"

The answer is simple: to awaken, to open your being.

Yes, we say 'simple' because for us it is simple. That is because polar bears have a simple walk through life. We face many challenges, but we are graced with a vast, open, quiet landscape. We are attuned to the energies of stars and sea and snow, the voices of ice and wind, mountains and lower earth, and star people too. We hold this space for the planet. As such, it is yours to share.

We feel this is an appropriate medicine at the current time for humans. In our view, humans may benefit from slowing down, from walking resolutely, with more focus upon who they are and where they are in relation to the Earth. Always relationship! Spiritual growth requires deep relationship with self—which is also to say a deep relationship with your world, Gaia, Mother Earth, the sky, sea, land, and all the peoples—four legged, two legged, no legged, winged and gilled, even jellyfish, upon the planet.

Humanity is at a very delicate balance right now, a precarious position. Our way is to encourage you. We offer an experiential 'seeing through polar bear eyes' as a way for humans to sense more sensitively, to feel your connection with all life more intimately, to know yourselves more wholly.

We bid you farewell for now and offer the idea to walk and feel the spirit of Earth greeting the soles of your feet as it speaks, through you, to your soul.

AN ENTICING JOURNEY

Every few weeks, I spent several hours rereading and contemplating my talks and dreams with the polar bears. I was well aware of their habit of presenting just enough information or hinting of new experience to leave me feeling both perplexed and intrigued. In this way they were excellent teachers, knowing the value of curiosity as a potent prod to further exploration, deepen investigation, and encourage self-discovery. For me, this often meant following divergent ideas, stumbling upon hidden patterns, and connecting dots not always apparent at first.

Reading over our last conversation, for example, I pondered the bears' emphasis on movement. Dream walking beside Bering was certainly an active movement, but so also was it very calming, a medley of motion and meditation. Even while conversing as we walked, I often felt myself open to a deep sense of stillness and communion—with Bering, the land, the sea, and the sky. I wondered if this was how it was for all polar bears, especially those dream walking through the Arctic landscape. It made me rethink the council's statement that we are all in this together. We may walk alone as individuals, but opening ourselves to the communion of deepened relationship we *know* that there is no other.

It is important for you to understand that not all polar bears consciously participate with our reality, clarified the council later that day. *Just as not all humans consciously participate in global awakening. In general, most animals are attuned to the universal flow and thus tuned in to deeper connections, but this is not always chosen for each individual life. Among some polar bears living today, the existence of our group is regarded in a mythlike manner, which is not to say untrue, but removed from their everyday experience of reality.*

Let us review: In the early times of our council's existence, we were only a few—simple Polar Bear people who joined forces in the dreamworld through a constellation of consciousness. We aligned ourselves, condensing our energies to create a space—what you might think of as a meeting place—for polar bears to gather and dream. The need was present, and those of us hearing the call responded, making ourselves available—first as physical bears and then in spirit form, as we moved beyond our physical lifetimes on Earth. We then sat on the council, to use a human phrase, and attuned in greater focus helping physical polar bears remember their dream connections and, later, recruiting humans to remember with us.

At present upon planet Earth there is the need for vast awakening. This is true for many animal species, but most particularly for humans. Humans have led the revolution, so to speak, in moving awareness away from inherent connection with All That Is so that they may remember again.

Why is this so? It is an enticing journey to re-find yourself, to see and know yourself anew. Much of what our planet is undergoing at this time is about seeing herself anew. In the midst of transformation there is chaos, a falling away so that the new may be born or created.

I thought of how this was true for me in smaller ways. Often when I traveled, even for a short period of time, I returned home with fresh eyes, remembering myself in a new way because I had stepped out of (or forgotten) my usual habits. This sometimes led to exciting changes in my life. Indeed, the movement away from myself to see myself anew was very appealing.

The Polar Bear Council has strived to hold certain threads of remembering so that the energy of connection can be recalled more easily. All over the planet—and under and above—different animal groups hold similar energies, just as some human groups have held energies designed for remembering, storing them in myths and songs and artifacts for others to find.

Let us acknowledge that there are many layers of consciousness on Earth at present. Think of it as many worlds coexisting. As surface people, humans tend to stay firmly focused upon one aspect of the world. Many animal groups are ahead of you in the sense of being able to traverse a multiplicity of worlds, to bridge layers, and access several dimensions simultaneously.

As you intuit, this is the gist of our dream work together. It is not by venturing faster or creating more technologies that awakening occurs for humans. Rather, it is by being still and silent, by moving steadily and resolutely upon the Earth.

This is the gift we bring to humans: a deeper sense of remembering, to remember all of your selves. So we begin to sing and tone and dance together, evolving together, all in One.

15

Arctic Is the Bear

The word *Arctic* comes from the Greek *arktikos,* meaning "of the North" or, literally, "of the bear." This pertains to Ursa Major, that large and prominent constellation visible in the Northern Hemisphere, which also contains the Big Dipper and points the way to Polaris, the polestar in the constellation Ursa Minor.* Stand northward of latitude 40° north, look upward into the clear night sky, and there you will see what the ancient Greeks saw shining brightly above them so many ages ago: a Great Bear, sauntering through the heavens.

Both Bering Strait and the council emphasized the polar bear's role in bridging Earth energy with star energy. They also shared their view that one of the key tasks of the polar bear species is to ground energies in the North, especially those needed for planetary awakening. As the council put it, *We hold a connection from the heavens to the Earth. You do not call us 'polar' bears without a reason, you know! Our job is to hold at the poles, and this is a very important job, one that has more significance than most humans realize. When you open to knowledge about the poles—magnetic resonance, cycles of shifting, and*

---

*An ancient name for Polaris was "the dog's tail," in reference to an early time when Ursa Minor (now known as the "Little Bear") was first viewed as a dog.

connections to stellar energies, then you are touching on our medicine in this regard.

One day the council suggested a more personalized view of this experience, an example of how ordinary polar bears interact with these energies as they live their lives. Bering Strait offered to share several *moments on the ice,* though as he noted, there are many versions of a typical day or night for a polar bear, for every situation, experience, and moment is unique.

Imagine yourself on an ice field under low skies in the season you call spring, Bering began as I opened my eyes to the Arctic dreamworld. *There is warmth where sun rays brighten patches of snow, while dark clouds hold other parts of the land in shade. The ice is melting and the air carries many scents. In some areas water and ice form a slush that is pleasing to polar bear paws on this particular day.*

I walk alone though I feel the presence of other bears. Some I see, but most I smell or sense with inner feeling. Some bears follow scent lines for food. There are seal lines and whale lines, and many more. We may follow the lines that other bears make, though we also have our own lines, some of which connect us to the energies and spirit beings of the land, sea, and stars.

I follow a line I know well. Following a line is like following a conversation. As I walk I deepen my being and extend my consciousness to connect with the people of the underneath waters. Think of them as a group of beings who reside below the surface of the water. They are many individuals—some living, some in spirit form—who coalesce their consciousness. With sharpened focus I can identify Whale, Seal, Walrus, Spirit of Water, and so on, but this is not to know their identity as a group. Just as I become part of a larger flow when I join with the Polar Bear Council, so these beings create a larger sense of being as they join together in shared awareness.

As I connect, I participate in their memories and shared knowledge. These seep into me just as my above-water vision, memories, experiences, and observations seep into them. It is through the soles of my paws that I 'meet' with them and they with me. Our connection is well established, so the line of connection is easy to find and follow.

Our connection is an ongoing relationship—not continually 'on' but always open. You might think of it similarly to communications you hold with animals. The ability to converse is present for you even though you may do other things throughout your day. Still, the connection is one you can tune in to whenever you like. It is up to you to choose when and how to attune—to hear the sound of the earth, to talk with various species, to connect with a particular being. In a similar fashion, this connection and relationship with the people of the waters and stars is always open to us (and to humans as well), and some bears find it soothing and pleasurable, not only to share knowledge but also to converse.

Many bears utilize these lines in practical ways, for specific information. But there are deeper connections too, and some of us form unique relationships. In this way we become specialists and help to widen polar bear understanding of these beings, as they share with us their views and experiences of the earth.

"And this information is then shared with the Polar Bear Council? And with living bears as well?"

All bears may participate. It is, as with humans, much a matter of the state of consciousness you engage in any moment. And yes, the Polar Bear Council receives updates from physical bears who connect with these lines and energies. All of this information is open and available. In many ways, this is what your Internet provides. Though we do not post ads or include false or misleading information.

Several animals I have spoken with have compared the Internet to the "inner net"—that vast, universal, telepathic network of shared information that can be tapped in to anytime, anywhere. In comparison, the Internet is a technological, outwardly manifest, human version of the inner net. It allows us to communicate instantly as well as share knowledge and immense quantities of information. Any human can contribute to our ever-growing cyberworld though, as Bering pointed out, humans do not always participate with the best of intentions. The many frustrations of the Internet—hoaxes, viruses, misinformation, cyberterrorism—reveal the shadow side of our species even as we strive to advance global consciousness.

Yes, agreed Bering. *This is a visual reflection for humans of the state of your intraspecies ability. If you cannot be clear within your own species, it will also be difficult to be clear with others, not to mention yourself. The world presents a reflection of who we are. This we understand and observe, especially in regard to humans. We do not know if humans observe this about themselves.*

When Bering or the council said things like this, I sometimes felt a weighty responsibility. How to open to a dialogue between humans and polar bears? How to share a story about polar bears that is so far removed from the general experience of most humans? How to convey their bridge of dreams, their deeper sense of connection between all beings that spurs us to evolve and expand our awareness?

We trust your abilities, the bears reassured me. *We support you, and we are willing for our story to be told through you. This polar bear dreaming book may take some time to ripen. It takes time to deepen one's being and walk with depth. It is your choice whether to take that time, to follow that depth of being. Where are you in your choices? That is a question for all humans—and an open invitation from us to learn more. We leave you with the image of walking upon the arctic ice. We send you a vision of great beauty as we walk, together, with you.*

NIGHT ICE

A few nights later, in the dreamworld once again, Bering reminded me of his offer to share "several" moments on the ice. This time it would be a group adventure, led by Bering, attended by the Polar Bear Council and myself. It felt good to join in common focus and exciting to experience a larger form of united dreaming.

In this moment we dream into the dark, polar night. We sense black sky, bright stars, and other planets too. Nimble streaks of red, blue, and green waves dance above. There is a silver sheen all over the land, and we walk amid such beauty.

Yes, polar bears appreciate beauty. We do not call it 'beauty' as such, but we feel a part of its presence as we walk through its midst. We participate in beauty. Almost all polar bears feel they are part of beauty all their lives.

There is a joy and peacefulness in such nightscapes. Many polar bears deeply appreciate our solitary walks in moments such as these. We do not feel lonely, for we are home within ourselves. We feel the connection of other polar bears nearby; we sense the whales swimming beneath our feet. We feel the distant presence of seals and walrus; our friends the arctic fox, who often follow us at a distance; and all the birds and fish. And we feel a connection to the sea and sky and ice and snow. As mentioned, we often attune to the underwater people or the sky and star people at these times.

These are sometimes 'meditative' walks, though we use that word loosely. It is not as if we are trying to meditate or sink into another state of consciousness; rather, it is an easing into a deeper sense of connection with all, with who we are. Our senses expand at such times, when we are not on the outlook for food or needing to be alert to changes in the weather.

Polar bears have few concerns other than food and movement. For us, movement is essential. Polar bears are generally not suited to zoos or cages; such bears must dream deep to remember their connections. We are deep creatures, however, so this is possible. We would even say that some polar bears do well in zoos.

These polar bears, by the way, often have a special connection to the Polar Bear Council. A polar bear caught in such a way is always contacted by the council within the dreamworld and offered a position, a window so to speak, that will allow other polar bears to learn the ways of humans. So also will this connection allow these bears to remember and participate in the larger world of polar bears. In this regard, we are a well-adjusted species; not all animal groups offer such an open window.

Let us return to our nightscape. Listen. So many sounds call to us! We listen to sounds upon the ice, within the ice, just under the surface and far below. We attune our ears to sky sounds, the calls of other animals that travel on the land, the songs of the whales, and more. Just as we feel lines of connection through our paws while walking on the land, so too we hear sound lines.

The whales also participate in such sound connections—creating, responding to, and following the sound lines that connect them not just underwater but, in a larger way, through a network that reaches to the sky people and well beyond. Polar bears are keen to observe this. We do not as a rule make these sounds and songs as whales do, but we have good inner hearing and are alert to the shifts and subtleties in such sounds. We also know how to ride sound lines in our dreams, and so journey to what you might call other dimensions—though they are not so much 'other' but simply another part of this planet in the universe.

The 'uni-verse' truly is one song, and that is what so many humans have forgotten. Just like many other animal groups, polar bears offer to remind you of our unique song so that you might recall your unique song and, in so remembering, more consciously participate in the One Great Song that lives through us all.

NEARING THE END

I felt it coming for several months—a slowing down of the talks, a settling of loose ends, a sense that the bears had shared all they wanted to share for the time being, and now it was up to me to put together their story.

My time with polar bears—from the initial invitation offered by a dream professor to meeting the polar bear spirits of the council, from the many adventures with Bering Strait to these ending talks—spanned several years. Even after the talks and dreams ended, this book took several additional years to write. As the Polar Bear Council noted, "It takes time to deepen."

In the last few weeks of our time together, Bering and I continued to walk through the Arctic dreamworld. I enjoyed these dreams immensely. In many ways they were similar to those in the very beginning—the seed dreams of silently walking beside the lone, quiet bear, yet I now felt myself as a very different dreamer.

I had learned to appreciate the subtleties of the Arctic dreamworld in a new way. I could identify the different calls of ice—high pitched; tinny and grating; hauntingly low like subterranean groans—with the associated meanings that polar bears assigned to them. I could sometimes hear the distinctive sound of seal breath at a distance, and sense them from even farther away. I learned to taste the air as polar bears do, opening my mouth just a sliver, lightly sucking in short pulls of air, allowing the scent to flow against my palate. I felt my senses loosening from their habitual pathways of interpretation and opening to new ways of experiencing. I realized that what the bears had once jokingly said was absolutely true: the Arctic will never be barren as long as there is Bear in the Arctic.

In one of our last dreams walking together, I noticed Bering suddenly stiffen in high alert. With that familiar toss of his nose, he indicated a turn to the left. We had been weaving our way through a jagged area of very large ice chunks, some big as statues, wide enough for a polar bear to hide behind. It was night, and the snow and ice glimmered with moonlight.

Halting behind an immense ice formation, eerily slick and translucent in the moon's glow, Bering nudged me back. Slowly, with what seemed to be just a bit of theatrical exaggeration, he peered around its edge.

"What?" I whispered. "What do you see?"

I watched his curiosity relax into amusement and, with a half step back, he allowed me to push forward and peer around his shoulder. There, in the near distance, a large polar bear—strong, substantial, self-possessed—meandered along the edge of an ice floe. He moved calmly yet deliberately, his fur shimmering silver white, his eyes closed as if dreaming.

You see me, said Bering.

A wave of hyperlucidity rippled through my body and for a moment I felt as crystal clear as bright Arctic air. The bear in the distance was Bering Strait, dream walking through his home. And here we were, awake in the dream, watching.

As my thoughts flashed back in time, I could not help but smile at this most fitting bookend to a strange and wonderful journey. I remembered how a big white bear walking beside me had once turned to look into my eyes, and how we *saw* each other in joined recognition, awakening to the dream.

Nudging me with his broad shoulder, as he had so many times before, Bering leaned my way. With a deep sense of well-being, I rested my hand upon his fur. And together we watched as the great white bear opened his eyes.

A FINAL WORD

Let us talk about deepening, and let us look at what you are most afraid of seeing: who you really are. This is one of the wisdom teachings that polar bears hold for humans. We know who we are.

We are a special people—strong and fierce, gentle and inquisitive. We choose to live where we do, away from the distractions and general busyness of the world.

We walk and hunt and raise our young. We taste the snow, listen to the wind, commune with the stars. And we dream, circling round the top of the planet, holding the world together.

We carry a message for all the Earth's peoples. Our message for humans is not about saving anything. There is nothing to save. There is only awareness—and awakening.

We recall to you a refrain from our first meeting: 'To be awake is to be aware of all worlds, just as it is to be aware of the sentience of all peoples—stones and stars, seals and polar bears . . . We wish to open pathways of communication between us. To open the lines of dream songs that encircle the Earth and unite us as the fellow beings in awakening that we are.'

Now it is time to share our remembering. We invite you to join us, to open your consciousness and walk beside us in the waking dreamworld, to move in to a new age of awareness and awakening, together.

With great love,

The Polar Bear people

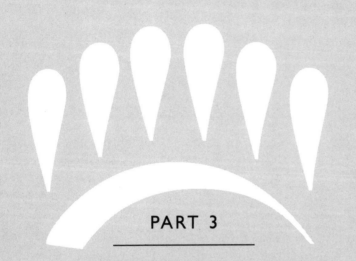

PART 3

Coming Home

Returning, you will remember your mission:
To serve the soul's remembering;
to go among people as dream ambassador
opening ways for soul to be heard and honored.
Let the world be your playground, not your prison.
Starchild, plunge with delight into the warm, loamy earth,
renew the marriage of Earth and Sky,
Follow your heart-light, dance your dreams,
commit poetry every day, in every way.
Now you are home.

ROBERT MOSS, "THE RETURN JOURNEY,"

DREAMWAYS OF THE IROQUOIS

16
Integrated Dreaming

One night, in the midst of drafting these final chapters, I had a dream.

I wake up in bed, throw back the covers, and walk outside my house to the front lawn. I lie down on the cool summer grass and look up into the night. It is unusually dark for summer in Alaska, and the sky is clear, ablaze with stars. Gazing in to the tiny, distant sparkles of light, I see windows in the sky—dark, diamond-studded portals that beckon and invite, granting access to the star people.

Happiness tingles through my body and I feel my back ease in to the earth. I am both surprised and comforted by how that gentle kiss of contact connects me with the energies of grass and soil and tree roots—a living, breathing membrane that holds our world together. I can sense deeper, too: clay and stone, water and bedrock, distinct energies harmoniously melded in the thrumming, pulsing planet that lies beneath me, supporting my body.

I am lucid, aware of lying atop the earth's skin, poised between the heavens above and the surge of deep world energies below. I realize this is what the polar bears meant when they shared about walking between worlds, bridging different forms of consciousness, serving as planetary conduits of energy and insight and wisdom. We are all this, I think—all of us, open doorways, living portals that link and bridge and allow movement between worlds—and a shiver moves through me. Such knowing feels good and strong and needed.

Then a small pop, as if my body cannot contain all that power—too much right now—and I am me again, a small human lying on her back, limbs outstretched on cool summer grass. I hear a noise and sense a presence. My body tenses—Is someone coming? I look around, stand up quickly, and walk back inside my house.

Every dream is a sacred journey, a potentially powerful, illuminating encounter with energies that call to us, reminding us who we really are. At the same time, dreams can be very practical, mirroring who we think we are right here and now. I loved seeing the distant windows in the sky, sensing the powerful surge of our Earth's interior, and feeling my place between the two.

Although I might have liked the dream to end on a higher note—a visit to the star people's abode, perhaps—I appreciated its honesty. I popped out of the state of expanded consciousness because the energy suddenly seemed too much, too big, too vast to contain. I heard a noise, wondered if someone was near—an outward projection of fear—and went back inside my house, back into the protective shelter of me.

Dreams are an impressive pathway to remembering ourselves home. And the dreamworld is amply accommodating, offering us a bounty of help throughout our journey—expert guidance, timely encounters, uniquely tailored challenges, and opportunities for mutual exploration and camaraderie. As the Polar Bear Council noted, "We offer this as a great learning lesson—to join with us in the dream is to awaken a bit, to begin to incorporate a larger view of consciousness so that remembering can occur."

WHERE ARE WE GOING?

Part 1 of this book was based on the experience that it's valuable to know the language of dreams, and beneficial to use a wide range of dream tools as we investigate the signs, symbols, hints, and clues presented to us from our inner world. Exploring the evolution of my bear dreams over several decades served to show how by making meaningful connections and opening gateways between our waking and dreaming selves, we deepen in relationship with the dream realm. So too, as we deepen in relationship with our dreams, meaningful connections are made and gateways open within us.

Part 2 was my answer to what can happen when we accept and follow an invitation offered from our dreams. It was an adventure in lucid awareness, shared consciousness, and co-dreaming with another species. We heard from the Polar Bear Council, explored meeting places that allow dreamers to converse, and considered various ways to shift consciousness so as to learn more about others and ourselves.

With part 3 we explore integration by looking at creative ways to work with our dreams and expand awareness—not only individually, but collectively, as a society, a species, a planet. Integration means bringing back what we've learned, using what we have discovered to forge new pathways, build bridges of conscious connection, and encourage each other to follow our personal signs, passions, and joy.

Throughout history, countless peoples of different cultures, religions, and species have embraced dreaming as a powerful vehicle to deepen connection with self and soul. For some, the dreamworld is the real world, the foundation from which our waking world derives. Dreams offer us all manner of gifts: messages from the spirit world, whispers from the higher self, yearnings from the subconscious, visits from alternate selves—even invitations offered on behalf of a Polar Bear nation.

This book began with an invitation—a folded note on fancy paper handed to me by a dream professor. Our dreams offer us many such invitations—and it's well worth our while to consider such offers. They are encouraging signs, often confirming that we have put some real effort into dream exploration and self-discovery. So, too, are they doorways to expanding awareness.

As the Polar Bear Council once put it, "You must first be opened, your door unlocked, so that a dreaming bear might slip in and take up residence. Perhaps he nudges you into the heart of a dream and shows you the life of a living polar bear. Then you begin to learn not just of the science or observation of polar bears, but how to think and feel and sense as a polar bear. This is the larger myth awakening."

Invitations are not always literal; they may come in the form of suggestions, tests, or recommendations. The Polar Bear Council once challenged me to locate their snow cave in the dreamscape and, later, to find the Meeting Place. Such invitations prompt us to heighten our awareness in the dreamworld by engaging us, by focusing our abilities on a particular task or skill. As the bears noted, these challenges are often an essential aspect of dream learning.

The invitation is always open. As the polar bears remind, "We have for a long time wished to connect in deeper ways with more humans; though, the timing is yours to acknowledge. We are available, we are open. It is for humans to ask, to humble their consciousness so as to see all that they do not see."

ARE YOU READY?

To start, we begin from where we are, here and now. For example, I am recalling the dream of walking outside my house, lying upon the summer grass, gazing up into the stars. I see windows in the sky, and feel earth energies flow beneath my body. I experience myself—and all of us—between worlds. What worlds? Heaven and earth; knowing and not knowing; everyday reality and altered awareness; the land of the waking and the cosmos of dreaming; and so many more. Integration is open to a multitude of paradigms.

One way to begin integrating a dream is to dream it again. We are often rewarded with greater depth and detail, additional insights, and, sometimes, expanded endings. Perhaps we naturally dream it again while sleeping. Or perhaps we open to it while waking. For me, this means centering, deepening, re-engaging the feeling of the dream. When I sense my ordinary consciousness sliding away and my inner eyes opening to the dreamscape, I know I'm there.

I wake up in bed and throw back the covers. I walk on bare feet through my bedroom, down the stairs, through the arched hallway, and out the front door. The air outside is both warm and cool; I can feel the lingering warmth of summer sun held by the earth, and the breeze of chilled mountain air. I lie on the grass, arranging myself in the same position as before. I look upward to see the same dark sky, the myriad stars, so tiny yet bright. My gaze relaxes and I see the windows in the sky, elegant cutouts that hint at something vast and grand.

If this was another kind of dream, I might imagine a ladder that stretches upward, a set of cosmic stairs that I could climb into the starry expanse and knock politely, hoping to meet the star people who live beyond the windows. "Another time," I tell myself, for this is not my intention for the dream.

I redirect awareness to my back, as I did before, feeling the buzz of my spine as it settles into the cool, springy grass. I sense the exuberance of earth forces that glide and swirl, gush and thrum just beneath the surface. And I open myself to the rush of energy that flows through me, becoming a conscious portal between heaven and earth.

And then—a pop, a noise, a presence. Breathing deep, I will myself to stay present, to face my fear. As I turn my head, I see the great white bear lying beside me. We reclined just like this on a snowbank in his Arctic home so many dreams ago. It's been over a year since I've seen him, and I am thrilled to meet him now, on my front lawn.

"It's you," I say, laughing at the obvious, yet heartened by the way my words convey the love and admiration I hold for the bear, and the great happiness I feel on seeing him once again.

We stand and walk together down the stone driveway, turning left onto the street. I notice how quiet it is, the dreamscape deserted, some houses lit from within, a few yellow porch lights shining dimly. The moon—a recent addition to the dream—shines bright. It's very peaceful and also . . . familiar. The scene is from another dream, one that occurred on the eve of my fortieth birthday when I asked for guidance to my future.

We walk to the end of the road and turn—as I did once before—to the left. Back then there was a forest at the end of the neighborhood, but now there is a subdivision. Times change in the dreamscape too. And yet the bear remains.

Emerging from the shadows, the black bear stops, stands upright, and regards us in silence. It's hard to read his expression—is he solemn, or amused? I wonder if he was a forerunner of Bering Strait, an advance messenger, a preview of things to come, or perhaps a guardian with a test, a challenge that may or may not have been met. Then again, perhaps the bear is Bering, another version, another self.

"It's you," I say again, as other possibilities also come to mind.

He is me, agrees Bering. But I am not him.

And for a moment I know exactly what he means. Poised in the pause between dreaming and waking, that little paradox makes perfect sense.

INTEGRATING SELF

Most every night we fall asleep and, without quite knowing how we do it, awaken in another world. Perhaps it's a world we know, or perhaps we find ourselves in a foreign land, a stranger in a strange situation. Most often, we don't know how we arrived—nor even that we traveled. We simply accept and interact with our dreams as if they are real because, of course, they are. And then, in the same uncertain way in which we began the journey, we return—back to life as we know it, awake in our bodies.

Dreams may surprise, scare, reassure, inform, enlighten, and inspire us. The dreamscape engages us with setting and ambience and a wide cast of characters, with mysteries and temptations and adventures, with story lines elaborate or simple, all uniquely tailored to meet our individual needs. We can't help but fall under its spell. The dreamworld speaks to us—personally and profoundly. Is this not an incredibly ingenious way of learning more about who we are?!

In the reality of the dreamworld, we live and love and learn. We may take advice from our many wise, capable guides. We may collaborate with dream partners, or share a laugh with fellow travelers. And we may begin to realize just how potent the creative power of our dreams can be.

Integrated dreaming is a balancing act. Like detectives, we hone our observation skills to find and decipher clues. Like artists, we delight in the power of symbol, the elegance of subtle connections. Like poets, we feel for the golden threads that sparkle and call to us in meaningful ways. As we integrate our dreams, we also integrate ourselves.

By engaging dream experiences energetically (not just thinking about them, but *feeling* them in exciting, vibrant ways), we travel with them, linking dreamscape with waking world. We may not even think of it as integration. Perhaps we are being like polar bears, curious and intrigued with unusual findings along our paw lines. Investigation beckons, nudging us, *Go on, have a look!* Opened by the spirit of playful exploration, we awaken to the dreamworld and recognize ourselves.

17
Dreaming with Animals

Early in our relationship, Bering Strait announced that he was a living bear—a mature male polar bear roaming the far Arctic, and a specialized dreamer. "This means I have certain skills in extending myself through the dreamworlds," he explained. "Many polar bears carry this medicine, though some to a greater extent than others. I am a special dreamer in that I am dreaming not only of polar bear evolution, but the coevolution of our planet."

Because of his abilities and connections with the Polar Bear Council, Bering Strait sought contact with a human dreamer to forge a deeper relationship between our species as well as a more conscious connection between all beings. "My job," he said, "is to help you to understand the world of the polar bear through our eyes; to understand the deeper vision we hold of both our kind, and our roles on Earth."

"This is not a new concept," he noted. "Many different animal species currently participate in this adventure. Some humans converse with animals and convey their feelings and insights; some share our stories; and some forge deeper relationships with animals, not simply from a biological, scientific viewpoint but as partners, friends. And there are humans who dream with animals, too."

My dream adventures with Bering Strait were tailored to our

individual personalities, common interests, and larger needs. The polar bears' desire to share their story with humans was paired with my ability to translate and write; my desire to learn more about dreaming was paired with the bears' ability to share their dream knowledge. There are many animals and animal groups that welcome similar partnerships with humans. As the Polar Bear Council emphasized several times, their invitation extends to all dreamers—"to engage in deeper, more authentic relationships with the Earth and all creatures."

The dreamworld encourages—and celebrates—such creative endeavors. Many animals feel it's easier to make first contact with humans in the dreamworld—and for good reason. Our guards are down, imaginations primed. When the heart is open, the mind is more accepting. In our dreams, we can do things that seem improbable or impossible in the waking world.

"Become a polar bear person," Bering Strait suggested several times. "Walk with us and dream with us and begin to live with us, within us, to see our world. That is the gist of our experiential gift to you: to see from our eyes." Indeed, one of the great benefits of dreaming with a partner is that we can share awareness; we can swap perspectives, try on different ways of being, experience new sensations—for example, what it feels like to move as a polar bear, to swim through Arctic waters, to shake one's body and shimmy.

When I followed Bering Strait to the lakefront gathering of hybrid human-bears, the dream hinted at what was to come. I resisted wearing the fluffy bear costume that was offered, but the bears nudged me on with humor. By putting on the costume, I accepted their invitation—and slipped into the skin and consciousness of Bear.

I recall the heightened sensitivity and novel perceptions, feeling deeply into the land through bear paws. I charged forward as a bear, powerful hind legs launching me into the lake. Awash in sensation, tickled by tiny bubbles in my fur, I felt supported by the dense layer of fat surrounding my body. How easily those strong legs and large paws propelled me through water! Diving deep, I swam through a portal and arrived in the Arctic. Kicking up out of the sea, pushing myself onto the floe, I unleashed a wild shake: energy rippling down shoulder, spine, legs, and tail; rotating fur, skin, and fat; flinging water everywhere—what a rush!

The dream engages us. Energizing us with emotions—amusement, awe, bewilderment, wonder—and sensations—running on land, swimming through water, heaving up onto an ice floe—the dream deepens us, changes us. We wake up and are changed as well. There is lasting power in such transformations.

The Polar Bear Council once related the story of a woman who dreamed of polar bear people. "She learned to walk slowly, to stop and see and listen and feel—not just with her eyes and ears but with her whole being. That in itself is a teaching for a lifetime! That is a return of wholeness to humanity, a gift from all animals, an opening to the fullness of planet Earth and beyond."

CO-CREATING

When I first met the Polar Bear Council, I was a bit intimidated. I slid into a student role, deferring to their size, wisdom, and authority. They encouraged me to take a more active role and helped me to understand that shared dreaming is a co-creation. The world Bering and I dreamed together was a meeting place between our waking worlds, a merging of our perspectives, experiences, and interests, something both created and discovered. When open hearts and unfettered imaginations join in the dreamworld, a new form of dreaming evolves.

The council reminded me several times that they had important reasons to arrange for a human and polar bear dreamer to meet: not only to share their story with humans but also to generate an experience, a creative example of what is possible, and inspire us all to dream large. It took me awhile to comprehend that they wanted me to help them write a book. When I finally understood, I had learned the importance of the question, what does the dream want of me? "Polar bears are not accustomed to writing books," the council remarked with their distinct, dry humor. "So, we enlist your services."

They explained that dreaming with other species is a beginning, a step into a greater co-creation. "Our aim is to walk with many humans—in your hearts and minds, to remind you of our co-creating ability. To move with us, to see through our eyes as we see through yours, that is the core of this book project as we see it: to open a conduit between our worlds, to allow vision and hearing and movement to create pathways, to link worlds that are not really so far apart—they are, in fact, the same."

"What do you want humans to know?" I asked. "What is your advice for readers who want to dream large, in co-creative ways?"

"Allow yourself to become vulnerable and open," they said after a thoughtful pause. "Risk asking questions and risk giving answers. Risk finding the deeper you. We offer you the movement of dreaming together, with us."

THE DEEPER YOU

Some dreams stay with us. Riding upon our wake of consciousness, they accompany us into the everyday world and we recall their story in full. Other dreams are more . . . dreamlike. They slide through the portal of wakefulness only to dash away, playing a game of hide and seek; they leave an image, a feeling, a shadowy memory peeping through everyday consciousness—and then, just as quickly, dissolving, disappearing. Perhaps such dreams are testing us; dancing just beneath awareness, they prod us to notice, feel, listen, remember.

Near the end of my time with Bering Strait, I had a special dream. I woke up with excitement, knowing I must write it down right away. But I had to hurry to the airport for an early-morning flight with my family. I spoke a few key words from the dream aloud as I got dressed, intending to jot them down as soon as I could. It was not until well into the airplane flight, however, that I remembered the words and the dream. All I had was a small notebook, so I wrote an abbreviated version with the idea that once we landed I could write the full dream in my journal. But I forgot. It wasn't until I returned to Alaska and, several weeks later, used the little notebook that I found the dream notes. This time I was in a restaurant, waiting for a friend. "No excuses," I told myself. "As soon as I get home I will rewrite this dream!" I tore the pages from the notebook, folded them in half, and placed them in my pocket. A week later, while doing laundry, I discovered the pages and—resolutely!—took them to my office. Once again, I didn't have time to rewrite the full dream so I carefully placed the notes inside the front flap of the big polar bear binder I kept next to my desk. And there they stayed for almost a year.

Some dreams are like that. They call to us again and again, in different forms, at different times, waiting for us to notice. Perhaps some dreams wait forever; perhaps there are some we never find. Maybe it's like this: when we finally do embrace a dream many times forgotten or misplaced, we are ready for its teaching. Then the dream shares what we need to know.

I live in a small apartment that is homey and comfortable, decorated with warm colors and vintage furnishings. I'm in the kitchen preparing a meal for Professor Behr, a visiting dignitary from another country. I'm nervous because he is famous and people are counting on me to provide good hospitality, but I'm excited too.

The doorbell rings and I rush to open the door. The professor is short, compact, and stylish. He wears a fedora and silk scarf and many layers of exotic clothing with rich colors—dark purple, ruby, maroon, and gray. His hands and face are covered with fine white fur. He speaks with a foreign accent, telling me he is, Hungry, hungry!

We sit at the wood dining table and I fill our bowls from a large tureen of bouillabaisse. I take one sip and already he wants more. This happens several times, until all the spicy fish soup is gone. With every bowl, the professor grows in size. He's now quite large, his clothes split open, fallen in tatters to the floor, and I see that he is thickly furred all over. "Ha ha, Professor Behr is really Professor Bear," I say to myself. "That must be why he is so famous."

The professor watches me intently. As I return his gaze, he tilts his head in a familiar way and I laugh, recognizing Bering Strait. "What a good disguise!" I exclaim. He jumps up and moves from room to room, exploring the apartment. He picks up objects—candles, crystals, little statues and carvings—sniffing them, turning them over, asking me to explain how they are made or used.

I follow him into an alcove and he points his nose toward a trio of framed black-and-white photos on the wall. I do my best to explain that these are made by a camera and special paper, light exposure and chemicals, but I don't really understand how photography works. Then he points to a phonograph and I notice bluesy jazz playing softly in the background. I tell him it's a recording, that people made that music a long time ago and a special machine formed grooves in a vinyl disc—the record—which can be played at other times, like right now. He paws at some old encyclopedias on a low book shelf. I take one out to show him the pages, explaining that people write down their thoughts and then a printing press places words on paper, and this is how we store these thoughts, in books. The more I explain, the stranger these objects and concepts seem—that we hold images and sounds and ideas in such ways to remind ourselves or allow us to relive them later on. It's odd, I think, but clever too. Memory markers, Bering says, *and my body tingles, as if we're on the verge of uncovering a secret.*

Hungry, hungry! *Bering says again, with the professor's foreign accent, and I recall the big bowl of chocolate mousse I made for dessert. I rush into the kitchen, excited to share it with Bering, and bring it into the living room.*

We sit together on a pillow on the floor, dipping hand and paw into the soft, thick, silky chocolate. As he eats, Bering hums in a way that sounds like yummm, yummm, *until all the mousse is gone, and the hum becomes a snore.*

I move my hand along his fur as he leans over and lies on his side. The fur is coarse but with each pass of my fingers, it becomes lighter and softer and smoother. Soon he is snowy white and much smaller, like a dog curled in slumber. I snuggle down to rest beside him and recall a similar scene from a dream long ago, nestling beside a big white dog on a pillow bed. I feel happy and at home.

AT HOME

Because so much of my dreaming with Bering Strait took place in an Arctic setting, this dream was special to me. I was heartened by the dream's warm, homey atmosphere, by the chance to share personal aspects of the human world with Bering—the wonders of photography and music and books, the joys of bouillabaisse and chocolate mousse.

The dream unfolds with one transformation and ends with another: The professor (a dream professor, a visiting dignitary, a friend incognito) eats bowls of soup, grows in size, divests human coverings, and reveals the bear inside. Later, he eats from a bowl of chocolate mousse, falls asleep, and through a magic touch becomes lighter, softer, smaller, a white dog on a pillow bed. "Hungry, hungry!" professor and bear each call before they change—a powerful invocation. Are they hungry for food, for knowledge, for fun? Are they hungry to satisfy their curiosity, or perhaps to wake the dreamer from the dream?

Maybe that dream took so long to settle into my conscious awareness for the same reason that explaining to the bear how human things worked caused me to see myself and my world in such an odd-feeling way, as if the familiar was suddenly strange and unusual. I felt myself teeter on the verge of knowing a secret, tingling with nervous excitement. The same feeling was present in the beginning of the dream, as I anxiously awaited the professor, hoping to make him feel at home. In the end, the professor—who is the bear, who is the dog, lies close in slumber. Something returns; a feeling lingers. I am happy and at home.

Although I don't live in a cozy apartment with vintage furnishings, the description fits me well. When conferring with Bering about details in this book, I mentioned this dream and said, "You know, that's not really where I live." *That's okay,* he remarked cheerfully. *That dream was not really council approved.* And together we laughed, for a good long time, like two little kids getting away with something big.

As we move from dreaming *about* animals to dreaming *with* animals, we forge deeper relationships not only with our dream partners, but also with ourselves. Journey far enough with another species and we inevitably rediscover our own. Not only do we open ourselves to more creative, expanded ways of dreaming in such partnerships, but we blossom in awareness, embracing, encompassing, inhabiting a larger presence of who we really are.

18
Dreaming Ourselves Awake

As a child I was fascinated by my dreams. It wasn't until my late teens, however, that I became intrigued by the process of dreaming. I read many books on the subject and enthusiastically gave myself assignments: to find my hands, to fly, to become lucid, to view my sleeping body from the dream state, and so on. Sometimes I was purposefully vague in directive, curious how my dream self would interpret the request. One time I asked to meet the "creator of dreams." Several nights later, I dreamed I was driving my car through a large parking garage.

The garage is dark and has low ceilings. The farther I go, spiraling down around the perimeter of each level, the darker and more compact the garage becomes. Finally I arrive at the very bottom. There are no parked cars, but in the middle of the open area there's a small office. Warm, golden light shines through the floor-to-ceiling windows. I go inside. It smells of oil and grease and is a bit messy, like most auto mechanic shops. Three short, spry, elderly men wearing matching shirts and amused expressions welcome me. I remember I'm on a mission to find the creator of dreams. One of the men nods, as if they have been waiting for this, and points to a bright yellow bumper sticker stuck at an angle, high on a wall behind them. It reads:

WE DO CREATIVE DREAMING!

I am surprised that three old men at the bottom of a parking garage are responsible for putting together such finely tuned, artful creations as dreams. Reading my thoughts, the trio smile affectionately. "We are the mechanics of dreaming," they explain.

On waking, I felt a surprisingly deep connection and fondness for the three lively old men. At the time, I was in college pursing a degree in symbolic anthropology and comparative religions. I found it telling that before the dream I probably would have envisaged a wise, white-haired magician or dancing, golden-skinned goddess to represent my creator of dreams—certainly not a trio of car mechanics working in an underground garage. And while I understood that *mechanics* of dreaming weren't necessarily *creators* of dreams, I instinctively knew how appropriate and fitting they were for me.

I visited the dream mechanics on several occasions, sometimes with a problem or purpose in mind, other times not, but always happy to see them. They smoked cigars, sat in swivel chairs, put their feet up on the counter, and told humorous stories that offered hidden advice. Whereas past dream experiments helped me to learn through experience, the dream mechanics opened me to relationship. The dream brought me home, to a deeper place inside myself.

THE PEP BOYS

Three decades later, I shared this dream with Bering Strait. I was lucid, and we were walking in a calm, meditative way. With Bering's help, I had recently accomplished the Polar Bear Council's task of locating their floating cave in the dreamscape. Perhaps I recalled the dream because the way the council's ice cave emanated light reminded me of how the mechanics' office glowed in the dark garage. Or perhaps the deep-down affection and trust I felt for the dream mechanics was similar to my feelings for the polar bear spirits sitting in their cave, assigning me tasks, helping me to better understand the mechanics of dreaming.

As I finished telling the dream to Bering, I recalled a related incident—something I had completely forgotten in the waking world. About three years after first meeting the dream mechanics, I went on a road trip through several southern states. While on the trip, I discovered the "Pep Boys"—Manny, Moe, and Jack—the caricatured personas of the founders (and name) of an automobile accessories store chain. Although it seemed silly, the Pep Boys reminded me of my dream mechanics; that they sold auto supplies only reinforced the connection. With a mixture of curiosity and amusement, I stopped to walk through one of the stores. I looked for something that might call to me or provide a link to the dream. But nothing seemed appropriate, and in the end all I took from the store was a free matchbook with the Pep Boys' logo: three smiling mechanics wearing bright yellow jackets, the same color as the bumper sticker in my dream.

Several weeks later, after returning home, I dreamed that I was in the parking garage, telling my dream mechanics about the Pep Boys. As I spoke, I put my hand in my pocket and felt the matchbook from the store. When I pulled it out and gave it to the mechanics, they exclaimed loudly and made a show of shaking my hand, as if to thank me. I was delighted they were so pleased.

As I related this second dream to Bering, I suddenly realized the significance of what had occurred—I had transported an object from the waking world into the dreamworld! Maybe the mechanics hadn't been shaking my hand to thank me, but to congratulate me. For years I had been so focused on remembering dreams, attempting to carry image and story line from the dreamworld into waking life, that I hadn't appreciated how we might also bring pieces of the waking world into our dreams. The realization inspired me to imagine—to dream—that I had the matchbook with me now. Without thinking how this would be possible, I reached into my pocket, felt for the cardboard booklet as I had with the mechanics, and pulled it out to show Bering.

I burst into laughter, really quite astonished with myself, excited by this magic trick of dreaming. As I wondered if I could do it again—was it truly this easy?—I noticed Bering bunching up his shoulders in small heaves, imitating the way I shook while laughing. This only caused me to laugh harder, and Bering accommodated by rolling his shoulders, exaggerating my movements, heaving his body to and fro. The hilarity was exponentially contagious, and I awoke on a tidal wave of laughter and bemusement.

DREAM LINES AND STAR SEEDS

Humor is often a gateway, and laughter a powerful energy that can shake loose our thinking and open us to deeper feeling. So many things had seemed funny in that moment: the cartoonish Pep Boys; the echoed magic of pulling the matchbook from my pocket; Bering Strait's playful imitation of my wonder and incredulity. The confluence of those dream events is a good example of what can happen when by following our dream lines we encounter meaningful connections, hidden pathways of consciousness, and unexpected bridges between the dreamscape and waking world.

When I first thought of my decades-old dream and related it to Bering, I opened a dream line—a track of dreaming, what the polar bears sometimes called a paw line. As I recalled the dream elements in greater detail—the parking garage and bumper sticker and three sprightly old men—we retraced the distinct curves of the line's route. It led to a memory—the road trip and the Pep Boys. By engaging the memory, we opened a conduit between worlds, and a second dream was recalled.

Sometimes traveling on dream lines is a connect-the-dots journey.

We don't always know where we are going. Perhaps the line first appears to be "just a dream," but as we walk it with depth and feeling, attentive to subtle connections and openings, we discover it is so much more.

My dream line led to a bit of magic in which a matchbook was plucked from the waking world, pulled through a pocket into the dreamworld. This happened not just once but twice—a double dose of matchbook magic. Repetition calls us to attention. "Look at me!" the little matchbook calls. And perhaps we notice, *Ah, there's something important here!* Every matchbook holds its own form of magic, after all—twenty potential strikes of fire dormant within a simple fold of cardboard.

In the end, magic brings astonishment and laughter. Funny how it happens, and contagious too. In the dream, the big white bear plays along, elevating the joy of discovery, the thrill of wonder and inspiration, the delight of shared adventure.

When we are inspired we are *in spirit,* suddenly opened to our larger presence. Pay attention to your field of dreams—Look! Listen! Feel!—and the dream lines shimmer before you. As Bering Strait once related, the easiest way to become a conscious dreamer is to follow your dream tracks, those lines of dreaming that speak most powerfully to you.

Once, while walking with Bering, I wondered how he first found his dream line. Was it different for bears than humans, or just different for each dreamer, no matter the species? I wasn't so much asking for an explanation as feeling for a connection—a sense of how it began for this unusual bear, the specialized dreamer who walked beside me. As I did not voice the question, I did not expect an answer, but as we moved together a wave of tenderness passed between us.

Then—in the middle of a step, in the middle of the Arctic dreamscape, a memory unfolds in front of me. I understand this is a special sharing, something unplanned and personal.

I see Bering as a young bear, no longer a cub but not yet on his own. He huddles asleep with his mother and sister in the curve of a snowdrift, while his dream body walks across the flat white land. He stops, tilts his head, listens to something I cannot hear. He moves his body in a precise way—a special movement, I understand—and, with a delicate push of his back foot, sails upward, into the dark, starry sky. He moves in slow motion, gliding smoothly, a dreamy, fluid dance of loops and spirals. His body glimmers silvery white, translucent against that black velvet sky, and everything feels impossibly close and connected. He floats in the luminous sea and stops before a tiny sparkle of a star. Ever so gently, he taps it with the tip of his claw. Ting! A musical tone that is also a frequency of light resounds, and the star splinters into tiny crystals—star seeds—that flutter to the ground and shine.

And then—we are walking just the same as before, as if we have not traveled one inch in distance, nor one moment in time. Bering snorts gently as he sometimes does, and I rest my hand on his shoulder. We continue to walk side by side, following a dream line that I can see, a trail of star seeds shimmering in the snow.

This is how it is, I think, as I now remember the feeling of that dream. Sometimes such a fragile, gentle magic nudges us on, one small thing leading to another. We follow dream lines each in our own way, as clues within the mystery prompt and beckon, reminding us every so often: *Yes, you're on the right track; Yes, this is really how it is.*

Maybe we stop and share an encounter with a fellow traveler, discover a bridge of connection, move through a gateway of awareness. Maybe we're always doing this—traveling dream lines that connect worlds not as separate as they seem.

FLUID DREAMING

Writing this book was like following a dream line. I didn't know where it would lead when we began; I didn't even know it would be a book. It started with a dog named Little High Top, a dream professor in an airplane, and an invitation. Acceptance led to walking beside a polar bear in the Arctic. Over and over we walked within the dreamworld, a synchronization of movement and consciousness, until at last one night the dream cracked open. We *saw* each other, and a conversation began. One thing led to another: a council of bears and a dreamer named Bering Strait; shapeshifting and shared awareness; meeting places and open doorways; a woman and a bear, walking together, awake inside a dream.

"Polar bears are not accustomed to writing books," they said, so I arranged our talks and dream experiences. Most appear in chronological order, only a few adjustments made for flow and the ease of your traveling pleasure. For *that* was also the point: to invite others on the journey, to follow a dream line together, to share some unusual events and encounters along the way.

We have walked beside a very special bear, our journey set in motion by a council of spirit bears who long ago imagined creating a dream bridge with humans. While drafting the manuscript, I was aware of the council's presence, sensitive to their desire of "working together to make a dream path visible." I often felt Bering Strait peering over my shoulder, nudging me in his good-humored way, offering a warm paw of support.

The polar bears do not consider dreaming separate from their lives. Think of it as "fluid dreaming," they suggested, "for it moves with us as we move throughout our life, day and night."

Humans can also become fluid dreamers, conscious dreamers who glide elegantly through layers of reality, dream ambassadors who carry the energy and insight and wisdom of our unique experiences into the waking world. Opening ourselves, embracing our connection with all life, we rediscover "the lines of dream songs that encircle the Earth and unite us as the fellow beings in awakening that we are."

It seems so simple, walking beside a polar bear in your dreams. Yet all the while the dream is deepening you—aligning your body with the meridians of the Earth, your thoughts with the patterns of the stars. By following the dream line, you are changed. Do you feel it? Perhaps you have become a polar bear person, not the same as you were before.

Follow your dream lines with an open heart and mind, and you will discover power spots, doorways of connection, bridges between worlds, energy portals that reveal ancient wisdom and future possibilities. Dream mechanics tinker in the golden light that shines from the basement of your being, polar bear dreamers dance in the dark starry sky above, and all of us walk together—laughing, loving, learning—dreaming ourselves awake. Welcome home.

Tips for Dreaming

I. SET THE STAGE

Launch your dreams with style, in ways that are meaningful to you. Before going to bed, state your desires: to recall dreams easily, to be lucid, to dream of a special person or place, to obtain guidance. Dream invocation can be simple (thinking about what you want) or elaborate (writing a letter to your dream guides, creating a dream altar). On waking, take time to review dream details—events, characters, landscapes, images, and messages. Respect your dreams and the dreamworld will honor you with more.

2. KEEP A DREAM JOURNAL

Essential equipment for any dream explorer! The act of physically writing helps to ground our dreams in waking life. Dream journals serve not only as records of where we've been and what we've experienced but also as foundations for further dialogue, bridges that help to link ordinary consciousness with the dreamworld. Use titles, sketches, or one-line summaries for quick recall and easy location later on. Even if all you remember is a fragment—a single image, thought or feeling—

be patient and record what you have. Sometimes we need to sit with a dream until it is ready to speak to us.

3. CULTIVATE CONNECTIONS

Become a friend and partner with your dream self. Request assistance from your dream guides. Ask for a one-on-one with your inner dream advisor. Pave the way for meaningful connections by cultivating good relationships. In the waking world, consider joining a dream group or finding a partner to share dreams. Connecting with other dreamers is a great way to learn more, offer and receive support, and gain fresh perspectives.

4. OPEN DOORWAYS

The Polar Bear Council recommends noticing how we enter and exit our dreams. It is good advice, for observing shifts in consciousness between waking and dreaming increases our awareness of such transitions and helps us notice other doorways within dreams. Such portals may appear as bridges, tunnels, turnstiles, chimneys, elevators, mirrors, gateways, and so forth. Some take us within, others take us through. Sounds, smells, or special movements can also act as doorways. Sometimes they lead to the sweet spot of the dream, where deeper meaning unfolds. Doorways may also act as triggers to lucid awareness.

5. PLAY WITH PATTERNS

Observe echoes and repetitions within dreams. These may be obvious (a phrase repeated several times) or subtle (a white stone, a white statue, a white plaza). Consider both the overall design and progression of your dream—do you notice a pattern in the way events unfold? Use your dream journal to discover recurring objects, characters, or topics that connect dreams. Pay attention to repeating dreams as well as ongoing themes that evolve through a series of dreams.

6. FACE YOUR FEARS

What shocks, embarrasses, or makes you feel uncomfortable? Notice fears, areas of uncertainty, and aspects of the dream you *don't* want to explore—they are often our untapped gold mines. Is something missing or unresolved? Some dreams help to bring a lost, hidden, or forgotten part of ourselves home so that we may become whole. Ask questions that frighten you. What is it that you are most trying to hide? Be willing to explore beyond your comfort zone.

7. PONDER, QUESTION, CLARIFY

When pondering interpretation, be vast; consider everything. Use books, films, and the Internet to research a character, place, time frame, object, or event. Utilize a dictionary, dream dictionary, or (often very illuminating) dictionary of etymology to jump start ideas. Be alert to puns, both verbal and visual. If you're stuck, draw a map of the dream or lay it out on a storyboard. Brainstorm as many different symbolic, literal, mythic, metaphoric, personal, transpersonal, and global associations that come to mind. Think outside the box. Trust gut feelings and intuitive hunches, but be open to alternate ideas and multiple (or multilayered) interpretations as well.

8. ENGAGE YOUR IMAGINATION

Do you wonder why a dream character spoke or acted in a particular way? Consider reentering the dream. Use meditation, shamanic journeying, or the power of your imagination to converse with dream characters, re-dream alternate endings, or follow divergent paths within a dream. Try viewing your dream as a play, film, or DVD. Make use of slow motion and zoom for added clarity. Interview the dream's director for behind-the-scenes commentary. Be creative! Imaginative dreaming allows us to uncover hidden perspectives and appreciate our dreams in larger ways.

9. BRING IT HOME

After gathering evidence, gaining insight, and pondering interpretation, bring deep meaning home. Shift focus from head to heart. Allow ideas and emotions to settle inside yourself. Consider that the meaning of a dream may change with time or become more significant as you grow in awareness. Sometimes it's wise to let things simmer.

10. HONOR AND TRUST

The more attention we give to our dreams, the more the dreamworld responds. Forge good relations with your dreamworld and keep pathways open to develop trust. Be patient and honor the natural unfolding of meaning. Some dreams are like time-released potions; they'll bring key insights or synchronous support when we need it most.

Tips for Co-Dreaming

1. READY THE FOUNDATION

To build a strong dream partnership, lay a strong foundation. Start at home. Be familiar with your dreamscape, in good relations with your dream guides, cognizant of how dreamworld symbols, events, and stories unfold for you.

2. FEED THE GUARDIAN

As a child I was promised the magic of flying—if I was first willing to open my closet door. While some dreams invite us to enter larger frameworks of reality, there may be guardians at the door. Perhaps we will be required to face a fear, perform a task, or expand awareness before we are ready to enter. Similarly, some dream animals test our persistence, patience, and resolve before sharing their secrets.

3. MEET YOUR MATCH

My match with Bering Strait was based on mutual interests, available connections, and common needs. Many animal groups welcome similar dream contact with humans to work together in co-creative ways. If interested, state your desire. Use meditation or inner world journeying to put out the call for an appropriate match. Be clear about who you are and receptive to who shows up.

4. BE PRESENT

Deepen dream relationships with presence and authenticity. Lead with an open heart and mind. It's okay to be vulnerable. What happens then? As the Polar Bear Council once told me, "We protect you, support your endeavors, and share our wisdom, too."

5. BALANCE

Co-dreaming develops and matures through mutual respect, trust, and participation. Work in tandem with your dream partner to confer and collaborate. Share your skills and insights; ask for help or clarification when needed. Find balance in dream relationships by learning as well as teaching. As the bears put it, risk asking questions and risk giving answers too.

6. USE WHAT WORKS

The dreamworld enlists our imagination to convey, translate, and share experiences. For example, we might share memories via projected films or holograms. We can communicate telepathically, through synchronized movements, or with parallel or superimposed vision. We can slide from individual views to group consciousness, or tap in to specialty areas (such as ancestral connections) when needed. Flex creative possibilities and open to a greater range of experience.

7. SHARE AWARENESS

Shared dream awareness may inspire us to try on different sensing modalities. With the help of the polar bears, I learned to sniff aromas with ursine sensitivity and hear the voice of the Arctic ice. Some animals allow us to share consciousness—to sit in the passenger seat of their sensory awareness. Or, we may become an animal, assuming its form and presence. Shapeshifts within dreams are useful templates to shifting consciousness in waking life.

8. RETURN THE INVITATION

Perhaps your dream partner would like to see the world from your perspective? Consider a guided tour, a visit through the apartments of your being, a shapeshift of the human kind. Represent the human species with good hospitality; serving chocolate mousse is a plus.

9. OPEN TO FULLNESS

Hungry, hungry to know more, to travel beyond conventional frameworks of reality? Learn to fly, bilocate, extend your consciousness in distance or time. Ask your dream partner to share and teach favorite modes of travel or perception. Use your experiences to bring expanded perspectives and new ways of being into the waking world.

10. DEEPEN CONNECTIONS

As the polar bears say, "the more you connect with us in dreams and participate in sharing thoughts, the more deeply we merge our consciousness with yours." Dream often and deepen connections. Sharing thoughts in dreams prompts similar experiences in the waking world. You may become more intuitive and telepathic, more sensitive to the feelings of others—and yourself.

Tips for Bringing Dreaming Awareness Home

1. FOLLOW DREAM LINES

Follow the trails that speak to you. Dream lines may lead to forgotten memories, alternate realities or time frames, and encounters with different aspects of self. The more we journey and explore—sinking into dreams, carrying messages back into the waking world, acting upon wisdom—the deeper the heart paths of connection. All dream lines inevitably lead home.

2. TRAVEL WITH DEPTH AND FEELING

As the polar bears note, humans may benefit from slowing down and deepening our connections with earth and self. Take time to engage your senses fully. Whether in dreams or waking life, a journey is more than just where we go and what we see, but the level of awareness with which we travel.

3. ANCHOR CONSCIOUSNESS

Be alert to images, objects, phrases, and encounters in dreams that also show up in the waking world—and vice versa. Memory markers not only reveal connections between worlds but also remind us of our multidimensional nature. Create your own markers by intentionally anchoring consciousness in an item that exists in one world and locating it in another.

4. DREAM WHILE WAKING

I sometimes saw the Arctic landscape superimposed on waking reality while daydreaming as a passenger in cars or boats. With a gentle shift of focus, I learned to step in to the dreamscape and engage a waking dream. Play with shifting awareness via relaxed vision, rhythmic movement, steady breathing, or daydreams to discover the entryways that open for you.

5. WAKE WHILE DREAMING

Dreams present a creative variety of links to waking awareness. Make use of synchronicities, unusual encounters, transformations, portals, or feelings of déjà vu to "wake up" within your dreams. Trigger lucid awareness by saying a key phrase, locating a specific object, or moving in a particular way to remind yourself that you are dreaming.

6. SWITCH PERSPECTIVES

What would happen if we viewed our dreams more literally and waking life more symbolically? Consider practical actions you might take to apply dreamworld insights in waking life. Use dream interpretation techniques to explore patterns, themes, and symbolic content of everyday events and encounters. Switching perspectives often helps us perceive underlying forces at work and thus more deeply appreciate our experiences.

7. EMBRACE THE TWILIGHT ZONE

Spend time in the twilight zone between wakefulness and sleep. Drift in and out of dreams; let yourself linger in the borderland. The more comfortable we become with liminal states of consciousness, the more at home we are in the in-between.

8. WALK BETWEEN WORLDS

Keep dream pathways clear, open, and well maintained with frequent travel and attentive care. Practice moving consciously and intuitively—relaxed yet aware—between the dreamscape and waking world. Imagine you are traveling in both simultaneously. Watch edges blur and boundaries fade. As the polar bears remind, "these worlds are not really so far apart—they are, in fact, the same."

9. BE INTREPID

Be an active, conscious dreamer, a keeper of dreams, a dream ambassador. Engage the power of dreamworld stories to motivate, inspire, encourage, and energize. Share your dreams and become a springboard, helping others to find and follow their dream lines. By recalling our unique song, we "more consciously participate in the One Great Song that lives through us all."

10. JOIN THE DANCE

Dreams bring us home. "Remember yourself with the dance of all creation," suggest the polar bears. Help facilitate authentic, conscious connections with all beings by being who you are. Join the dance. It's not the same without you.

Notes

CHAPTER 2. THE BEAR IN THE CLOSET

1. Rainer Maria Rilke, *Letters to a Young Poet,* trans. Stephen Mitchell (New York: Vintage, 1986), 84. This is an abbreviated quotation from Rilke's Letter Eight, written August 12, 1904. Mitchell's translation reads: "We can't say who has come, perhaps we will never know, but many signs indicate that the future enters us in this way in order to be transformed in us, long before it happens."

CHAPTER 3. FACE TO FACE

1. Brunke, *Animal Teachings,* 64.
2. Andrews, *Animal-Speak,* 251.

CHAPTER 4. THE POWER THAT HUNTS US

1. Moss, *Dreamgates,* 160.

CHAPTER 5. DANCING WITH THE POLAR BEAR

1. Hillman, *Dream Animals,* 32.

CHAPTER 6. ARCTIC DREAMERS

1. Brunke, *Animal Voices; Animal Voices, Animal Guides; Shapeshifting with Our Animal Companions; Animal Teachings; The Animal Wisdom Tarot.*
2. Brunke, *Animal Voices, Animal Guides,* 228.
3. Ibid., 229.
4. Ibid., 230–31.

CHAPTER 7. THE POLAR BEAR COUNCIL

1. Brunke, *Animal Voices, Animal Guides,* 14.

CHAPTER 8. ENTERING THE DREAM

1. Buhner, *Ensouling Language,* 28.

CHAPTER 9. WHAT WE KNOW AND WHAT WE DON'T KNOW

1. Ovsyanikov, *Polar Bears: Living with the White Bear,* 46.
2. Ovsyanikov, *Polar Bears,* 50.

CHAPTER 13. THE HUMAN–POLAR BEAR ALLIANCE

1. For more on this, see chapter 2 of *On Thin Ice* by Richard Ellis.

Bibliography

Andrews, Ted. *Animal-Speak: The Spiritual & Magical Powers of Creatures Great & Small.* St. Paul, Minn.: Llewellyn Publications, 1997.

Bluestone, Sarvananda. *The World Dream Book: Use the Wisdom of World Cultures to Uncover Your Dream Power.* Rochester, Vt.: Destiny Books, 2002.

Brunke, Dawn. *Animal Teachings: Enhancing Our Lives through the Wisdom of Animals.* London: CICO Books, 2012.

———. *Animal Voices, Animal Guides: Discover Your Deeper Self through Communication with Animals.* Rochester, Vt.: Bear & Company, 2009.

———. *Animal Voices: Telepathic Communication in the Web of Life.* Rochester, Vt.: Bear & Company, 2002.

———. *The Animal Wisdom Tarot.* London: CICO Books, 2013.

———. *Shapeshifting with Our Animal Companions: Connecting with the Spiritual Awareness of All Life.* Rochester, Vt.: Bear & Company, 2008.

Buhner, Stephen Harrod. *Ensouling Language: On the Art of Nonfiction and the Writer's Life.* Rochester, Vt.: Inner Traditions, 2010.

Ellis, Richard. *On Thin Ice: The Changing World of the Polar Bear.* New York: Alfred A. Knopf, 2009.

Granath, Fredrik. *Vanishing World: The Endangered Arctic.* New York: Harry N. Abrams, 2007.

Hillman, James. *Dream Animals.* San Francisco: Chronicle Books, 1997.

Moss, Robert. *Active Dreaming: Journeying Beyond Self-Limitation to a Life of Wild Freedom.* Novato, Calif.: New World Library, 2011.

————. *Dreamgates: Exploring the Worlds of Soul, Imagination, and Life Beyond Death.* 2nd ed. Novato, Calif.: New World Library, 2010.

————. *Dreamways of the Iroquois: Honoring the Secret Wishes of the Soul.* Rochester, Vt.: Destiny Books, 2005.

————. *Here, Everything Is Dreaming: Poems and Stories.* Albany: State University of New York Press/Excelsior Editions, 2013.

Ovsyanikov, Nikita. *Polar Bears.* Stillwater, Minn.: Voyageur Press, 1998.

————. *Polar Bears: Living with the White Bear.* Stillwater, Minn.: Voyageur Press, 1996.

Turner, Victor. *The Ritual Process: Structure and Anti-Structure.* Ithaca, N.Y.: Cornell University Press, 1969.

Waggoner, Robert. *Lucid Dreaming: Gateway to the Inner Self.* Needham, Mass.: Moment Point Press, 2009.

PLEASE SEND US THIS CARD TO RECEIVE OUR LATEST CATALOG FREE OF CHARGE.

Book in which this card was found _____

☐ Check here to receive our catalog via e-mail.

Company _____

☐ Send me wholesale information

Name _____

Address _____ Phone _____

City _____ State _____ Zip _____ Country _____

E-mail address _____

Please check area(s) of interest to receive related announcements via e-mail:

☐ Health
☐ Ancient Mysteries
☐ Spanish Language

☐ Self-help
☐ New Age/Spirituality
☐ Sexuality/Tantra

☐ Science/Nature
☐ Visionary Plants
☐ Family and Youth

☐ Shamanism
☐ Martial Arts
☐ Religion/Philosophy

Please send a catalog to my friend:

Name _____ Company _____

Address _____ Phone _____

City _____ State _____ Zip _____ Country _____

Order at 1-800-246-8648 • Fax (802) 767-3726

E-mail: customerservice@InnerTraditions.com • Web site: www.InnerTraditions.com

INNER TRADITIONS
BEAR & COMPANY

Inner Traditions • Bear & Company
P.O. Box 388
Rochester, VT 05767-0388
U.S.A.